WAR AND THE HUMAN RACE

WITHDRAWN

UNIVERSITY OF CALIFORNIA, LOS ANGELES
FACULTY LECTURE SERIES   1968

War and the Human Race

Edited by
MAURICE N. WALSH

ELSEVIER PUBLISHING COMPANY   *Amsterdam London New York   1971*

ELSEVIER PUBLISHING COMPANY
335 Jan van Galenstraat
P.O. Box 211, Amsterdam, The Netherlands

ELSEVIER PUBLISHING CO. LTD.
Barking, Essex, England

AMERICAN ELSEVIER PUBLISHING COMPANY, INC.
52 Vanderbilt Avenue
New York, New York 10017

Library of Congress Card Number: 78-135481

ISBN: 0-444-40901-7

Printed in The Netherlands

To the memory of

ERNEST JONES

a pioneer in the study of human aggression

Contributors

Bernard Brodie, Ph.D. Professor of Political Science, University of California, Los Angeles.

Herbert Friedmann, Ph.D. Professor of Biology, University of California, Los Angeles; Director, Los Angeles County Museum of Natural History, Los Angeles.

John Kennedy, Ph.D. Associate Director, Department of Social Psychiatry, Center for the Health Sciences, University of California, Los Angeles.

Jere C. King, Ph.D. Professor of History, University of California, Los Angeles.

Maurice N. Walsh, M.S.M.D. Associate Clinical Professor of Psychology, University of California, Los Angeles; Senior Instructor, Los Angeles Psychoanalytic Society and Institute, Beverly Hills, Calif.

Walter Wilcox, Ph.D. Professor of Journalism, University of California, Los Angeles.

Contents

Hartmann —

Editorial Introduction

MAURICE N. WALSH

The urgent need for a scientifically based, multidisciplinary approach to an understanding of the recurrent plague of war prompted the organization of the University of California, Los Angeles, Faculty Lecture Series of 1968 on the subject of "War and the Human Race". The organization of this series is also a recognition that this holocaust of mankind is almost the last great plague that needs to be subjected to this kind of approach, which has in the final analysis been responsible for their solution and disappearance except for mass hunger, pollution of the environment and racism which, like war, also urgently need such an approach.

An objective examination of the problem of recurrent mass homicide, commonly called "war", will demonstrate the confusion which currently exists on every level in regard to this phenomenon. Cliché judgments, patently unscientific and untrue statements and deliberate attempts to confuse, abound. As far as international attempts to regulate international violence and aggression are concerned, it is evident that, in spite of the existence of the United Nations and in part due to attempts to destroy its potentially beneficial influence, there still exists among nations a virtual state of international chaos.

In fact most larger nations appear to operate their international relationships, particularly with smaller nations, on the same blundering and aggressive basis as the person in Louis Carrol's famous couplet:

"Be sure to beat your little boy,
Every time he sneezes.
He only does it to annoy,
Because he knows it teases."

The series "War and the Human Race" takes cognizance of the fact that any fruitful approach to the complex problem of recurrent mass homicide must be both multidisciplinary and scientifically sound. Naive and oversimplified approaches have not only failed to solve the problem in the past but, as Professor Brodie's contribution demonstrates, have confused it. The Faculty Lecture Series of the University of California at Los Angeles, given in the fall of 1968, thus represents a pioneer endeavor in this regard.

The contributors include a biologist, an anthropologist, a historian, a political scientist, a psychoanalyst and a professor of journalism who was himself a front line soldier. More than one of the contributors have experienced military

1

service in the combat zone themselves and thus can speak from first hand experience from their participation in the mass holocaust of World War II.

Any discussion of homicidal behavior in man must necessarily begin with a consideration of his biological nature, that is his basic make-up and the nature of his inborn impulses and instincts with which, like other animals, he is endowed. Pope's well-known 18th century aphorism "The proper study of man is man" should be expanded to suit the circumstances and state of knowledge of the 20th century, in order to replace this now antiquated and limited point of view, it would then read "The proper study of man is nature and man's place in nature as a part of nature".

There is now no doubt that man is the product of a long and complex process of evolution from simpler organisms, nor that he carries within his nervous system simpler and primitive types of nervous organizations, which are overlaid, and to some degree controlled, by more recently developed and higher nervous controlling organizations.

As might be expected these later developed and more complex nervous structures and functions are not always successful in controlling the behavior resulting from the activity of earlier and more primitive types of nervous organizations. The brilliant 19th century English neurophysiologist Hughlings Jackson was the first to demonstrate that in human beings higher and more complexly organized neurological mechanisms have been added progressively and in an evolutionary fashion, so as to control simpler and more primitively organized neurological structures; which still, however, exert their primitive functions under the control of higher centers and at times are liable to escape the higher control of the more recently organized brain centers.

Man is essentially without biological weapons of offense or defense except for his brain, which is the largest and most complex of any mammal. It has often been erroneously stated that, because man has brain centers and mechanisms for the expression and elaboration of both aggressiveness and sexual behavior, inevitably the human is condemned to irresistibly repeat mass murder and rape in generation after generation. As will be demonstrated this is an oversimplification, a cliché which can do nothing but retard understanding. There is now no doubt of the existence of brain centers, in the phylogenetically more ancient portions of the human brain known as the hypothalamus and the cingulate gyrus of the temporal lobe, for the expression and elaboration of emotion. For many years neurologists and neurosurgeons, notably Sjöquist and others, have noticed that brain tumors in the region of the third ventricle, *i.e.* the hypothalamus, have produced the phenomenon of "sham rage". This phenomenon was correctly attributed to damage to centers controlling aggression, thus releasing primitive aggressive behavior.

Cannon (1929) suggested that the hypothalamus of the brain mediated the emotional life. It was, however, in 1937 that Papez, on the basis of neurophysiological studies, demonstrated that the hippocampus, its efferent tract the fornix, the mamillary bodies, the mamillo-thalamic tract, the internal nucleus of the thalamus and the radiation of its inferior nuclei to the cingulate gyrus all constitute a mechanism for the elaboration of emotions. The observations of Klüver, Bucy, MacLean and others that stimulation in the region of the amygdaloid nuclei evokes vigorous behavior associated in the human with strong fear and anger, as well as the clinical observations of Penfield, Gibbs and others, indicate that in the temporal lobe and hippocampus functions related to the affective component of behavior are elaborated.

The work of MacLean and others, who have employed electrical stimulation of the hypothalamus, has demonstrated that stimulation of areas a few millimeters distant from the areas which provoke behavior associated with strong fear, anger and sexual behavior will provoke the opposite behavior, thus indicating the existence of centers for inhibiting the preceding behavior. As a result of these studies we now have the important information that there exist in this phylogenetically ancient portion of the brain centers both for the expression and the inhibition of aggession as well as sexual behavior.

There can be little doubt that these findings indicate the existence of inborn mechanisms for the expression and the inhibition of both aggressive and sexual behavior. The existence of higher inhibitory centers in the human cerebral cortex for the inhibition of both behaviors indicate that higher, more complex, and more recently organized centers for the inhibition and the control of these biologically and phylogenetically primitive and ancient instinctual activities are present and are important in their control.

The fact that there exist multiple centers for the inhibition of expression of these instinctual drives indicates both the strength and the difficulty of their control as well as the necessity for mechanisms for emergency control to avoid, if possible, the violent and potentially destructive breaking out of these primitive instinctual drives. Psychoanalytic studies, which cannot be reported in detail here, indicate that within the human temporal lobe of the brain there also lie structures which have the function of matching percepts with preconscious as well as unconscious repressed memories and fantasies, with which are associated psychic derivatives of the primitive drives.

In 1923, Sigmund Freud produced his dual instinct theory, thereby creating a landmark in human history. He postulated that there exist in the human, as in other living creatures, two basic instinctual drives: namely those of *libido* and *aggression*. He presented a mass of evidence to show that both instinctual drives usually occurred fused together, and that in regressive psychic states such as psychoses and certain types of neuroses and criminality, they tended to become defused, aggression then appearing in its most naked form. This situation is most graphically seen in individuals suffering from psychoses and in criminals, in which the individual under the pressure of his uncontrolled instinctual drives may indiscriminately commit murder and rape. Because of the extreme complexity of the human psyche, however, this situation is not limited to psychoses and criminality alone. Deviations from the normal control of both instinctual drives occur in a variety of psychic disorders, including neuroses and also certain perversions.

Should we be discouraged by the biological fact that there exist, built in as it were, certain brain centers for the expression of aggression? I should like to again call attention to the fact that there also exist in the human brain centers for the *inhibition* of aggression, which are of equal importance to those for its expression. In fact we find in the anatomical structure of man centers for the expression of both tendencies. In addition there are in the human cerebral cortex the highest centers for the inhibition of aggression. In actual life experience the difficulty is seen to be one of control of the primitive tendencies which tend to escape from inhibition under numerous situations. The important question to be answered from the scientific standpoint, therefore, would be, "Under what conditions do these primitive aggressive and destructive instinctual drives escape from higher control, and how can we learn to reinforce the inhibition without the drive being turned against the individual himself? ". This is a most important question and one which merits the most carefully thought-out and highly organized research projects which can be devoted to its solution.

It was for this reason that the present Faculty Lecture Series has been organized, essentially in order to provide approaches to an understanding of the problem from the standpoint of many disciplines — a recognition that the question is a difficult one and one which will require the best efforts of many scientific specialists for its solution.

The researches of the psychoanalytic school of psychology, initiated by Sigmund Freud and carried out by his successors, demonstrate conclusively that the type of intellectual education at present carried out in the institutions of higher learning of the world must be supplemented and added to so that in the future, with the accumulation of more knowledge, education in the field of human emotions must be granted an equal place with intellectual education. The persistence of the fallacy that the conscious portion of the human psychic functioning constitutes its entirety has delayed recognition of the basic importance of the unconscious portion of the mind, a persistence of the childhood type of mentation into adult life, which far outweighs the conscious functioning in quantity if not in quality. This means that the majority of the adult human psychic activity is of unconscious origin and is therefore more or less childlike in its nature. This dangerous situation can only be corrected by making the unconscious psychic functioning conscious, a most difficult task and at present one which is only possible through psychoanalytic therapy.

Therefore intensive research into mass techniques for achieving this aim must be considered to be of the utmost importance. At this point in history it is impossible to state whether or not such an aim can be attained in the future. However, as in all science, the final answer to the problem can only be determined by intensive and well-organized research into the problem.

We can conclude that a long and complex biological evolution has been responsible for the development of the present complex structure of the human brain as well as the human psyche. In fact this has represented an ascent of man from animal barbarism. Periodic regressions into barbarism, appearing as recurrent episodes of recurrent mass homicide or of endemic criminality, regrettably persist and are responsible for a huge amount of human suffering and death. The phenomenon of recurrent mass homicide still constitutes a plague of mankind similar to the great plagues which in the prescientific era afflicted the human race, a prominent example being the recurrent episodes of bubonic plague which, transmitted by rat fleas, were responsible for millions of deaths and for the destruction of the health of many more millions until it was eliminated by the application of the scientific method, in recent times.

Through the application of the scientific method these plagues of humanity, with the present exception of the plagues of recurrent mass homicide, mass pollution of the environment and mass hunger (to the solution of which the scientific method is only beginning to be applied), have entirely disappeared from the earth, and the suffering produced by them has been largely forgotten. Attention is called to the fact that in their time they too were considered hopeless of solution except through mystical appeals to the gods, an appeal which was never answered by any solution of the problem whatsoever, which had to await the advent of the scientific method for their final conquest.

Professor King, the historian of the present series, reminds us that the historian can no longer claim to present a unique and authoritative theory of the origin of war as was formerly assumed. Indeed the historian in former times was the first specialist to concern himself with this problem and, as might be expected, his approach tended to be unidisciplinarian and thus limited. However, it should be recalled that one of the first historians to consider the problem in ancient times, namely Plutarch, wrote a psychological analysis of the character of Alexander the Great which was penetrating for its time. Thus we early see in the work of Plutarch a need for a psychological understanding of the pathologically charismatic human leader who drives his people into mass episodes of recurrent homicide.

We are reminded by Professor King that any consideration of the problem of war (mass homicide) must include a knowledge of contemporary factors operating to touch off such holocausts as well as of episodes of this plague which have occurred in the past about which accurate historical information must be available for critical study. He notes the compliant and uncritical cooperation of many scientists with political and military leaders in the creation of ever more horrifying weapons, with a total moblization of national resources, which began in World War I and was brought to near perfection in World War II. This has culminated in a "military socialism", with its accompanying dangers to education and civilization. The lack of an international, effective world police force can thus lend apparent logic to the professional military men's statement that the present, enormously wasteful, expensive and threatening military establishment is necessary and desirable.

The fact that the entire biological world, with the possible exception of its human component, is an amoral one (right and wrong failing to exist as ethical values, as Professor Friedmann notes) must give us pause. Can we also claim that because man is a part of biology and that the biological world is essentially amoral, that man too must be condemned to be amoral? The fact that amoral men do exist need not be doubted. However, modern psychiatry, immensely enriched by the psychoanalytic studies in depth of the human personality, its

5

illnesses and its deviations, informs us that in the human amorality is essentially a function of psychic abnormality. It can only signify a deficiency on the part of the reality testing and regulating functions of the ego as well as a deficiency in the prohibitive and idealizing functions of the superego or conscience structure.

It is thus impossible, as Professor Friedmann the biologist of the series observes, to compare a human killer with a predatory animal which kills for food and in which aggression shows no signs of extinguishing its own species. On the contrary, aggression in predators tends to maintain the balance of nature by keeping down prolific non-predators.

The demostration by Morley in 1953 that both ants and humans, as the two most successful creatures capable of existing in almost all of the life zones of the earth and both now existing without important predators, prey upon and make war in an organized manner upon others of the same species is of basic importance. There can be no doubt that in their earlier history both ants and humans did suffer from the attacks of dangerous predators which threatened to extinguish their respective species. However, through evolutionary development a state has been reached in which both types of creatures are free from important predators.

It can be no accident, however, that, this being the case, both ants and humans alone among other living creatures make war upon and destroy others of the same species. This biological fact would tend to indicate that the aggressive instinctual drive in living creatures, in the absence of important predators, can be turned against the species itself and can thereby become destructive even though its original purpose was adaptive and protective of the species by mediating and organizing defense against predators. The aggressive instinctual drive, Professor Walsh maintains, was originally adaptive and protective against attackers and predators of other species. The fact that in humans and in ants, in the absence of important enemies, it can be turned against the same species would indicate that we have here *a deviation of the aggressive instinctual drive:* in the sense that its original biological purpose is no longer needed but continues to operate as a senseless impulse to the detriment of the same species which it was originally intended to serve.

But can the same really be said of human beings? This is a question which merits our most serious concern. It is now quite universally recognized that the superficial and naive statement that war maintains the balance of nature in humans in the same way that predators do in the animal world is a myth, since the present studies show that the expression of naked aggression, manifested through the destruction of other human beings, is largely led and initiated by psychologically abnormal individuals.

One can say with certainty that the time-honored human habit, unfortunately not rare, of placing nations under the control of psychologically abnormal, aggressively perverted persons, together with the modern factor of the ever-increasing new invention of massive weapons of destruction, is certain to be suicidal for the human race unless interrupted. This tendency of societies to select psychiatrically and pathologically charismatic abnormal individuals, of the nature of aggressive perverts, to control nations and to lead them into war indicates that intra-specific aggression in the human race has gotten out of hand and has become a serious threat to the survival of the species. This can only mean that natural selection in the human is being interfered with, and that unconscious forces, basically responsible for the existence of aggressive perversions as well as for the uncanny ability of such pathologically charismatic individuals to seduce normal human beings into selecting them as leaders and following them to the death, can effectively upset the balance of human nature and can brutalize and destroy human beings *en masse* with enormous damage to the painfully attained process of civilization.

It is significant that both the biologically trained lecturers in the series, namely Professors Friedmann and Walsh, agree as to the existence of an aggressive instinctual drive, which they consider not merely to be a reaction to mere frustration. Professor Friedmann, in common with many biologists, feels that the aggressive instinctual drive is basically beneficial to the species, in that it enables the individual mammal to resist attack and even to avoid conflict.

It cannot fail to be significant, as mentioned above, that the two most successful types of creatures, namely ants and humans, which at present have no important enemies or predators and which exist in almost all of the life zones of the earth, are the only two types of creatures which make organized mass attacks called "war" upon others of their own species. It is a fact that certain species of ants make organized "war" or attacks upon colonies of their own species for the purpose of stealing food and young individuals, and of making slaves of the conquered, very much as do humans. It would appear that the aggressive instinctual drive in ants and humans, since they have no present need for protecting themselves against other species, may in effect be turned blindly against individuals and groups of their own species. It is well-known to psychoanalysts that, in the human, instinctual drives may be deviated and perverted and turned to the destruction instead of the protection of humans; and we have here a social example of the deviation of an instinctual drive from its originally protective function.

An important function of political science, as exemplified in the contribution of Professor Brodie, is the dissipation of age-old myths and fallacies regarding human society. The constructive questions regarding human society and mass homicide which are asked by him are also of great importance. Some of them have been answered in his own contribution and in contributions of the other contributors, namely those of the biologist, the anthropologist and the psychoanalyst; others remain to be answered, and final answers can only be forthcoming through more intensive research.

The brutal and amoral mistreatment of small nations by larger nations has gone on since the start of recorded history, and probably can be traced back to the destruction of smaller villages by well armed groups from larger villages or by groups of marauding nomads. Nevertheless, one finds modern, supposedly civilized nations indulging in this amoral practice and rationalizing these outmoded, obsolete, amoral and totally indefensible attacks on smaller nations which are carried out ostensibly for "defense" but actually for the purpose of trying out new weapons and methods of warfare. Military men particularly appear to have little difficulty in rationalizing such savage international behavior which, after all, gives them a chance to put into practice the techniques of destruction and aggression which they have been trained for; although the original and supposed purpose of these techniques was for the defense of the homeland and of the homes of the people. The psychological defense mechanism of *defense by attack* can be unconsciously placed in the service of a perverted aggressive drive, and, through clever and seductive propaganda, populations can be led by a pathological charismatic leader to believe in the falsehood that their lives and liberties are in danger.

As un unfortunate result the unhappy inhabitants of small nations have been up to the present time repeatedly attacked, maimed, destroyed and savagely misused, and their children have been deprived of parents while they have, themselves, been maimed, burned and killed. Their women have been prostituted and their means of livelihood repeatedly destroyed, leading to mass undernutrition and starvation, with damage to young nervous systems and minds.

Professor Brodie notes that the contribution to the understanding of the human psychic processes made by psychoanalysis must be applied to the problem of international violence and armed conflict. The persistence in the human unconscious of primitive barbaric concepts, popularly thought to be obsolete, constitutes one of the principal obstacles to any solution of the problem. For example, the largely unconscious relegation of aliens speaking another language to an inferior or subhuman status permits them to be ruthlessly mistreated and killed without a conscience reaction on the part of the aggressor. For those who doubt the existence and power of such survivals from barbarism it is only necessary to remind them of the widespread nature of this tendency, as shown by the recent Nazi myth of the "Master Race" and of the tendency of American troops to refer to members of alien and Asiatic peoples as "gooks", who are then regarded as beneath contempt and can become the objects of aggression.

This ethnocentric tendency is familiar to anthropologists, who find in all primitive peoples a strong tendency to regard their own tribe as the only human group. This is often designated by a name for their fellow tribemen meaning "The People", such as the Esquimaux name "Inuit", the Navajo name "Dinné" and the Hopi name "Hopishinimu" for people of their own tribes, other peoples being regarded as less human and therefore as barbarians.

Included in the present series is a contribution from a former combat front line soldier, Professor Wilcox, now a professor of journalism in the University. He notes several facts which can be corroborated by anyone who has served in the combat zone, including the present writer. The peculiar isolation of the front line soldier makes him feel apart from other men and also has to do with his need to stay in the line and identify with others in the unit. His main preoccupation is to stay alive, and killing the enemy is the only way to do that, apart from making himself as inconspicuous as possible. He goes on because he must go on and do the task assigned to him by his society, since alternatives are so damaging to his self-esteem and to his social status, particularly in relation to his fellow soldiers. There is no honorable alternative for him, except the conquering of the fear of death and of his repugnance against killing others against whom he has no personal quarrel, sufficiently to fight or to be wounded or die. The high portion of the underprivileged of the population in the combat troops, noted by Professor Wilcox, has undoubtedly been significant in "wars" throughout history. These unfortunates bear an undue share of the affronts, indignities and stresses inevitably associated with war. The distresses suffered by these young men attract our sympathy and our humanitarian feelings. To condemn our youths in each generation to suffer such horrifying maiming, suffering, and death in a blind acting out of the evils of the society should arouse in us an impassioned desire to understand, once and for all, the basic roots of such an inhuman process and to halt it.

The anthropologist of the series, Professor Kennedy, remarks that "all intentional killing of men by other men is murder", and he notes the fallacious arguments of the functionalists that war might be culturally productive because of its supposed role in producing nation-states or its supposed adaptive function in consolidating and centralizing internal power, so that it is commonly considered in some vague fashion by naive individuals to be beneficial. The development of progressively more complex episodes of recurrent mass homicide from simple tribal and group attacks of men upon each other is graphically described by him.

The only hope of escaping such recurrent holocausts is through the application of the scientific method to their understanding and then to their solution. On the basis of facts brought out in this lecture series, the occurrences of outbreaks of mass homicide, or so-called "wars" on the average of approximately 19.56 years in most large nations over the last 150 years can be related to the following basic factors:

(1) A strong and largely unconscious hostility of older males against younger males resulting from the Oedipal situation, *i.e.* the early competition of the father and the son for the mother, plus the jealous need of the older male to preserve his position which is progressively threatened by the arrival of the younger male at sexual maturity in late adolescence.

(2) The unconscious persistence of recurrent mass homicide derived from and representing the initiation rite of primitives. The same factor, namely the now unsuspected and disguised initiation rite involving the murder, maiming, the infliction of suffering, a demonstration of courage and a contempt for death of new generations of late adolescents, is responsible for the society's adulation of military heroes, while those individuals who have distinguished themselves in the saving of lives are much less dramatically rewarded.

(3) The rise in each generation of aggressively perverted, homicidal but intellectually brilliant and pathologically charismatic leaders who, because of their unconscious need to express their perverted aggressive instinctual drive, move into power vacuums and take advantage of economic, sociological, and historical factors to seduce and deceive large elements of the population into following them. This usually results in the organization of the military for the attack on supposedly less strong populations of other nations, this being a con-

9

tinuation of the primitive "war game", a form of initiation rite. Leaders and followers of the opposition are systematically imprisoned, tortured, and murdered; and the nation is thus committed to a suicidal course resulting in its ultimate destruction together with the lives, healths, and property of millions of the people of the aggressively perverted leader, who frequently is either murdered or commits suicide when the destructive process initiated by him proves intolerable to his people.

This destructive social process can only be ameliorated or interrupted by an awareness of its existence, followed by the application of the scientific method to its understanding, and through a comprehensive, multidisciplinary, well-financed, organized and systematic research program finally brought under control. This effort will inevitably be opposed by selfish interests devoted to the perpetuation of the status quo, which, however, must not be permitted because it is not oriented to human welfare and can potentially result in the final destruction of the human species.

The time has finally come when humans must unflinchingly confront the phenomenon of recurrent mass homicide as a recurrent plague of mankind, only to be solved through multidisciplinary scientific research. This effort will naturally be opposed by demagogues and self-seeking politicians and military men who wish to maintain the status quo, i.e. the primitive and prescientific repetition of the wasteful and suicidal episodes of recurrent mass holocausts which have been predominant up to the present time. There is now no further need to disguise the factors which must be combatted in organizing such an effective research program and finally an effective preventive for this recurrent plague. The fact that its origins and meanings are complex should serve as a challenge rather than as a deterrent for such an endeavor. The saving of human life and suffering, as the highest human goals, should be paramount. Selfish, antiquated and obsolete interests must eventually give way before the impact of humanitarian endeavors.

The thanks of the contributors are extended to Professor Erik Walgren Ph. D., Professor of Swedish, UCLA and Chairman of the 1968 Faculty Lecture Series and to Mrs. Lillian Hays, Coordinator of the Faculty Lecture Series, for their unfailing helpfulness, kindness and support.

BIBLIOGRAPHY

Cannon, W.B., *Bodily Changes in Pain, Hunger, Fear and Rage; an Account of Recent Researches into the Function of Emotional Excitement,* Appleton, New York, 1929.

Freud, S. (1922), Beyond the Pleasure Principle, in J. Strachey and A. Freud (eds.), *Standard Edition of the Complete Psychological Works of Sigmund Freud,* Vol. 18, Hogarth Press, Londen, 1955, pp. 69—144.

Freud S. (1933), New Introductory Lectures on Psychoanalysis, in J. Strachey and A. Freud (eds.), *Standard Edition of the Complete Psychological Works of Sigmund Freud,* Vol. 22, Hogarth Press, London, 1964, pp. 1—184.

Hess, W.R., *The Functional Organization of the Diencephalon,* Grune and Stratton, New York, 1957.

MacLean, P.D., The Limbic System with Respect to Two Basic Principles, in M.A.B. Brazier (ed.), *The Central Nervous System and Behavior,* Josiah Macy Foundation, New York, 1959, pp. 105–116.

Morley, D.R., *The Evolution of an Insect Society,* Allen and Unwin, London, 1954.

Olds, J., Pleasure Centers in the Brain, *Sci. Am.,* 221 (1956) 105–116.

Olds, J., Differentiational of Reward Systems in the Brain by Self-Stimulation Techniques, in E. Ramey and D. O'Doherty (eds.), *Electrical Studies in the Curarethetized Brain,* Harper and Row, New York, 1960, pp. 17–51.

Penfield, W. and T.C. Erikson, *Epilepsy and Cerebal Localization,* Thomas, Springfield, Ill., 1941.

Sjöquist, O., Hypothalamic Discharge and its Relation to Epilepsy with the Respect of a Case of "Sham Rage" in Mice with Surgical Verification, *Acta Chir.Scand.,* 85 (1941) 235–249.

Theories on the Causes of War

BERNARD BRODIE

Nothing in the habits of man seems more ancient than war, nor more modern. This persistence is remarkable, because the very words "ancient" and "modern" conjure up fabulous changes in the environment — technological, cultural, and political. War itself has also changed, culturally as well as technologically. The pursuit of glory, for example, is not nearly so much a part of it as it once was, even recently. Nevertheless, there have remained throughout certain identifiable characteristics which justify us at least in using the same label, "war", to denote what we are talking about. Among these characteristics are an explicit sanctioning of very large-scale violence, which is practiced by well-organized groups, usually in a fashion ruled by convention and obedient also to certain well-defined circumscribing or limiting factors — for example, customs relating to the humane treatment of prisoners of war. Customary too are such remarkable traits as a clear ending — which separate periods of war from what are longer, usually much longer, periods of equally remarkable amicability.

It is easy to jump to the conclusion that this persistence of something which changes and yet remains identifiable as war only proves that there is something in human nature which requires it, or at least accounts for it. Well, perhaps there is. We shall want to examine this notion later on, but we ought to recognize at once that there are some cultures which do not practice or even know war, that even within our own nation-state culture there are some states which for all practical purposes never engage in it, and that those which do may have very long periods — 40 or 50 years or more — without war. Also, where war exists, it operates through and among many institutional and bureaucratic elements which tend to filter out the thing we call human nature. It is also obvious that certain other forms of human behavior, similar or dissimilar to war, have sometimes existed for extremely long periods of time only at last to disappear suddenly, or at least be modified out of recognizable relationship to the original custom. I have in mind, for example, such a custom as dueling, with its elaborate and rigid code, which happened to be an expression of human nature restricted mainly to the upper classes and which took a very heavy toll of these classes for many centuries.

Anyway, despite the persistence, frequency and extreme costliness of war, our knowledge of its basic causes is slight and marginal. Also, as I shall try to make clear presently, what purports to be knowledge is often a fabric of the most conspicuous error. Even more astonishingly, few persons seem at present even to be trying in any rigorous and systematic fashion to find out why men fight wars. There are, as there have always been, plenty of offhand declarations

12

about what causes war, most of them falling into a number of quite familiar patterns, but the real testing of one concept against another, insofar as it is possible to do so, seems presently to be out of fashion.

It was very much in fashion in the period between the two world wars, but in the academic or scholarly world practices and pursuits often go in and out of fashion for reasons that are not always rational or even identifiable. I am talking now about theories explaining or pretending to explain war as a phenomenon, rather than about the explanations given for the origins for particular wars. The latter is the work of historians, who, incidentally have tended to make the causes of particular wars appear a good deal more rational than was warranted by the fact that very fallible and usually mediocre men were responsible for tripping them off. Actually, a moment's reflection will suggest that it is rather difficult to find particular causes for any given war when we are so much at a loss to understand the underlying factors through which the particular ones must operate. Without that knowledge we may easily fasten our attention on the wrong things.

Those specific elements in a situation which one observer might consider of considerable importance are ignored by others, perhaps including the mass of historians, either because they think those elements are totally irrelevant or because they have been too little noticed. For example, from what I have read about Kaiser Wilhelm II, I should deduce that he was a man of pronounced homosexual tendencies, and that would seem to help explain certain aberrant aspects of his behavior prior to and during the crisis of 1914. Yet I know very few historians who have noticed that fact and fewer still who consider it relevant. I should not want to exaggerate its relevance or importance, but it may help account for the exceptional braggadocio and instability conspicuous in the Kaiser's character and in so much of his intervention in diplomacy. At least I can imagine it being as important in the world crisis leading to the guns of August as various other factors which have been much more noted.

I should like now to take up a number of general theories about causation of war which have been popular during the last 30 or 40 years. This theorizing can be fitted into four general categories: economic, psychological, political, and historical or specific. The last mentioned hardly belongs in this talk because I want to emphasize here basic causation of war rather than specific causes of specific wars. However, there is a tendency to find in some alleged causes of specific wars lessons of general applicability. For example, the naval race between Germany and Britain prior to 1914 is supposed to have played a major role in the causes of World War I, or at least of the British intervention in that war, and it therefore has been used ever since as a perennial example of the danger of arms races.

A kind of theorizing which was particularly popular during the twenties and thirties and which still has echoes today belongs within my "economic" classification, though it happens that few if any economists of stature ever attached much importance to it. It was a species of Marxian or rather neo-Marxian theory, though the people who advanced it most ardently, rarely considered themselves Marxians.

13

The original Marxian idea was that not individual capitalists but the system of capitalism itself was responsible for causing war. In the Marxian view, when all nations would be communist there would no longer be wars. During the Czechoslovakian crisis of 1968 we did, in fact, see one way in which war is avoided between two communist powers, that is by one moving in with such overwhelming strength that the victim considers it futile to resist. That is surely not what Marx had in mind, but perhaps we shall live to see a test of the true Marxian gospel in a confrontation between the Soviet Union and China. I hope not because I do not have that much interest in seeing a theory disproved. Nevertheless, the present tension between those countries is interesting for theoretical as well as tactical reasons.

However, the theory that was popular in the twenties and thirties was not Marxian in this aloof sense. It blamed not capitalism but rather some selected capitalists, particularly — though this was a somewhat later development — those entrepreneurs who were "merchants of death", that is to say manufacturers of arms and munitions. In other words, it was essentially a "scandal school" or "witch hunt" theory.

Those who wrote books and tracts in support of this thesis included some quite distinguished or at least well-known people. Perhaps the reader will remember the names of P.T. Moon, Harry Elmer Barnes, Charles Beard, and Walter Millis (who died only a few weeks ago), and of course Bertrand Russell. In general, this theory, if it can be called such, was an attempt to expose the hidden economic incentives of competitive imperialism which, as was well known or at least assumed, was the major factor in producing wars.

The pattern went something like this: A capitalist would invest heavily in some backward area, mostly to exploit natives and create markets, and when he encountered the competition of foreign capitalists, he would get his government to support him with threats or actual use of force. Naturally, the foreign entrepreneurs would do the same and the result would be a confrontation between governments. Sometimes it was not even the etrepreneur's own government that allegedly pulled the chestnuts out of the fire. For example Napoleon III was supposed to have intervened in Mexico in support of the claims of a Herr Jaecker, who was actually a Swiss national. Question: *Why* should Napoleon III have been so willing to stick his neck so far out in support of the claims of a Swiss? Further question: *Why* should he do so even for a French national? The "why" is after all important, and the answering of it should be part of the explanation.

There was a group of what were supposed to be well-known instances of like nature, such as the machinations of the Mannesmann brothers in Morocco, which were supposed to have greatly heated up the fires of controversy between Germany and France. There was also the Yalu River dispute in the Far East, in which Russian private investments in the Yalu River area were supposed to have touched off the Russo-Japanese War of 1904–1905, which proved so disastrous for the Russian monarchy.

Later on, as I indicated, the emphasis fell on the munitions maker. Walter Millis wrote a book called *The Road to War*, which happened to be one of my

14

assignments in a course I took as a graduate student and which explained the U.S. intervention in World War I primarily on the basis of the allegation that American munitions makers had committed themselves to heavy support of the Allies on a credit basis and then induced our government to protect their loans by going to war to prevent the collapse of the Allies. Our American Ambassador to Great Britain, Walter Hines Page, was supposed to have played an especially important role in this maneuver. To be skeptical of these explanations was to be thought simply naive.

In the late thirties, however, these theories began to take a real beating from the work of a few first-rate scholars who took the trouble to study some of the source material. One of them was the distinguished historian, William L. Langer, still flourishing I believe, who contributed an insightful and revealing book called *The Diplomacy of Imperialism, 1890-1902,* published in 1935. He discovered that the sharp rivalry of the European powers in the building up of their empires during that period was due to quite different motivations from those the demonologists described. Another significant author was Herbert Feis, also still flourishing, who wrote a very significant book called *Europe, the World's Banker, 1870–1914* (1930). Then there was Professor Eugene Staley, who I think is still active at Stanford University and who produced a book entitled *War and the Private Investor* (1935). It was Staley's teacher, Professor Jacob Viner (also, I am happy to say, one of my own great teachers), then at the University of Chicago, who became suspicious of the fact that it was the same well-worn cases that were adduced over and over again to prove the scandal-school interpretation of the chain reaction from private investment to national crisis. Under Viner's guidance — the book began as a doctoral dissertation — Staley began to look carefully into the facts surrounding each of the well-known cases and found that the results were almost invariably an inversion of the alleged pattern. That is, where entrepeneurs were involved in the internationally dangerous maneuvers abroad, it was usually their governments that had put them up to it in order to have what was at that time considered a respectable cover for governmental action. Thus, for example, it was the Russian court which was using for its own expansionist purposes those of its nationals who could be induced to invest in the timber of the Yalu River. Finally, there was that wonderful summing-up little book by the British economist, Lionel C. Robbins, *The Economic Causes of War* (1939), which utterly demolished the scandal-school approach for those who could read.

However, social science has the great disadvantage that its insights are conveyed by the use of words, sometimes many words, and usually badly written ones. Words of one author have to compete for attention with those of many other authors. Thus, even the best and most original works are often ignored. After all, Freud's greatest and most searching work, his *Interpretation of Dreams,* was originally published in only 700 copies which took years to sell. I think what really destroyed the scandal-school theory, at least for the thirties and forties, was the advent of Hitler and subsequently World War II. Though Hitler was in the beginning described as a front man for some nefarious German capitalists, this interpretation was soon relegated to the place it deserved. The

15

whole phenomenon of Hitler and World War II simply did not fit the theories which had been so popular. Even the attribution of supreme evil to the munitions makers, which had stimulated inquiries of the Nye Committee in 1934 and which had moved the head of the Du Pont family to declare that his firm would no longer engage in any kind of munitions manufacture because he did not want to spend the rest of his life proving that he had not caused the war which might come soon, tended to fall by the wayside.

Most unfortunately the old idea was given new life by the valedictory speech of President Eisenhower, where he warned his countrymen to beware of what he called the "military-industrial complex", without telling us either what he meant by the phrase or what that complex was supposed to be guilty of.

Obviously, there are companies which make products that the military use, whether arms or household goods. Obviously too, these companies want to sell their wares even if the chief buyer is the Government, which happens often to be a rather difficult customer to deal with. Some of those companies will engage in lobbying to be at least partly successful. That this kind of activity has ever had a significant effect on American foreign policy, however, particularly that kind of policy which might produce a war, is a consideration of quite different significance. Even Mr. Juan Bosch, whom one would expect to be very sensitive to such influence, declared after the unfortunate American intervention in the Dominican Republic in 1965 that he saw no indication that our intervention had been at all instigated by American financial interests.

Let us consider a few relevant and obvious facts. In the first place, companies in the same industry are usually competing primarily with each other. The firm known as General Dynamics was interested not only in having the Government buy what later became the F-111, but was specially interested in winning the contract over Boeing. Actually, Boeing was probably lucky to have lost the contract even though it spent $25 million in the reserach and development attendant upon making its bid. Second, the aircraft industry is rather exceptional in the degree in which its products are oriented towards military use. Yet even the major aircraft companies are primarily interested in cultivating their civilian rather than their military business. Most of the very large companies which are engaged in the production of some munitions are usually enormously diversified and have on the whole very little commitment to that portion of their business which is military. I am told, for example, that Dow Chemical Company, the prime supplier of napalm, devotes about 0.5% of its entire manufacturing effort to the production of that commodity. I am told also, and I fully believe it, that the company would be glad to be rid of its commitment to make napalm (its executives have undergone a good deal of harrassment because of it) but that it continues to engage in its manufacture mostly out of a sense of patriotic duty. Certainly Dow Chemical was one of the very many companies engaged in military production whose stock advanced with the sharp and prolonged rally in prices touched off by President Johnson's announcement of March 31st, 1968 that he was stopping the bombing of North Vietnam and inviting President Ho Chi Minh to engage in negotiations. Also, everyone on Wall Street agrees today that the end of the Vietnam war would have a further bullish effect on practically all stock prices (although this may already have been anticipated by the time it comes to pass).

The idea that the continuance of the war is considered good for business, and that this alleged result is responsible for its continuance, is a notion as ridiculous as it is disgusting, yet many people do believe it. In our university newspaper, *The Daily Bruin*, the following sentence appeared in an article of the election of 1968. It said about Mr. Humphrey, the day before he was defeated at the polls: "Moreover, his support of a policy of sending thousands of U.S. workers and students to die in Vietnam so that Mobil Oil, Bank of America, and many others could make fatter profits, shows that he is an enemy of the people". This notion reaches a special height of preposterousness in mentioning a bank, which is exactly the kind of financial institution which likes the war the least — the severe credit crunch of 1966 was hardly favorable for them — but in any case it is taken off a very dusty and antiquated scrapheap of discarded ideas. How much easier life would be for us teachers if we didn't always have to redispose of notions properly disposed of long ago!

It happens that we live in an era in which the most sensitive decisions of government are kept secret for hardly more than a matter of months. Books of memoirs which Meg Greenfield has described as the "kiss and tell" type, like those of Arthur Schlesinger, Jr., Ted Sorensen, Roger Hilsman and General Maxwell Taylor have revealed as well as criticized the actions of presidents and cabinet members still in office. Even General Eisenhower has given us some revealing memoirs of his tenure in the presidency. There are also numerous accounts, like that of the late Robert Kennedy in the posthumous book entitled *Thirteen Days*, where he describes in detail the emotional as well as calulating atmosphere around President Kennedy in the Cuban missile crisis. These are among the many nonclandestine ways of learning what is really going on, and there are a lot of industrious people scrutinizing the records and telling us what they find.

I have myself had some occasion in the past two decades to witness some of the decision-making process at moderately high levels in the departments of both State and Defense. I could prove what I have already stated and what it is not at all necessary to prove, namely that representatives of various industrial firms do a certain amount of lobbying to get contracts. But I have never seen or read or heard of the slightest real evidence of any intervention of financial or industrial interests with respect to such high policy decisions as those determining our interventions in Korea, Lebanon, Cuba, the Dominican Republic and Vietnam. This is the kind of influence which members of government would not let them have and which they have shown no desire to acquire. Nor do I remember seeing, hearing, or reading evidence of their stimulating or guiding in any significant respect policy decisions concerning procurement or use of various categories of armaments, including decisions involving the use or nonuse of napalm. The evidence to the contrary is not only impressive, but overwhelming.

To cite one specific example among innumerable available ones: it was not the (considerable) lobbying of North American Aircraft Corporation to sell their B-70 but the ardent desire of the Air Force to have that bomber system that Mr.

Robert McNamara had to contend with in denying it to them. Those who witnessed that epic battle at close range know that North American's propaganda was of zero influence on the chief contenders and certainly on the outcome.

I turn next to that group of theories which might be called psychological, or more precisely, psychoanalytical; if there are those among you who feel that we are now entering the area of pseudo-science, I assure you that I do not share your feelings. At this date one should hardly have to say so. The practice of psychoanalysis is now about 70 years old, which means it has had thousands of practitioners, some of them very brilliant indeed, and hundreds of thousands of patients. I mention this only because some of my remarks may seem negative about the field and about its practitioners, and I want it to be clear that my overriding feelings about both are certainly not negative.

It is probably true that excessive intellectual modesty is not an occupational disease of the psychoanalytic profession. They have very much indeed to tell us about human behavior, and it is too easy to believe that that is all one needs to know. I have heard speeches and read papers by analysts who purported to tell us why men love war and violence where I thought that the authors needed to know a great deal more about facts not readily available in the clinical offices where they spent so much of their time. Before we ask ourselves, for example, *why* men love war, we ought to be clear that they really do, and it seems to me that the evidence to support the notion that they do is very slender and subject to all kinds of counter-indications.

Unquestionably, human emotions, including and perhaps especially repressed emotions, are a terribly important part of the reason why men resort to war, or being in an obviously unprofitable war, find it so difficult to withdraw from its clutches. Emotions affect perception as well as decisions and behavior, and they certainly affect the degree of rigidity we show about any of these. No doubt there is a good deal of aggression in the normal human being, especially the male human being, and no doubt there is also much repressed rage in some neurotic personalities who occasionally rise to commanding positions of power. There can hardly be any doubt that these factors are involved in the genesis of wars and in accounting for the intensity and especially the persistence with which they are often fought.

However, it is also obvious that war is a rather poor form of outlet for human aggression or rage. It has long been much too dangerous and too costly, and the object or intended victim is too impersonal and remote. Aggression and rage are always more suitably taken out on visible, tangible persons close at hand, who have a significant relationship to oneself, especially if the means of retaliation are circumscribed or limited. Also, it is more satisfying not to have the intervention of enormous policy-directed bureaucracies to overorganize the job, which is what happens in war. Besides, emotions like anger are usually pressing in their demand for fulfillment against a target. The man who is struck across the face needs to strike back at once. If hours or days must intervene before he can do so, he is likely to have second thoughts and to balance his original motivations against considerations not originally potent.

I am especially unimpressed by the current (though by no means new) habit of drawing analogies from the agrgressive or otherwise antisocial behavior of animals. Animal behavior as compared with that of human beings has at least the benefits of relative simplicity and frankness of exposure, but until I see the counterpart in animal life of government bureaucracies, of customs and traditions by which foreign policy and other objectives are determined and pursued, and the ability to predict easily certain gross consequences from the reciprocal use of such gadgets as nuclear weapons, we are clearly wrong in pressing analogies too far.

There is also the simple and hard to negate fact that different political regimes do have conflicting objectives and interests, however, foolishly or shrewdly those objectives and interests have been determined. Also, while the determination of the subjects to pursue those interests even through war clearly draws power from the emotions, it draws strength also from intellectual conviction, which again may be faulty but is not necessarily psychologically irrational. I am speaking, for example, of the conviction of President Ho Chi Minh that Vietnam ought to be unified under the control of himself or his party, and that of three American Presidents that in this objective he should be opposed. Surely their minds have been fixed on the goals rather than on the expression of aggression.

In an article in a recent issue (November, 1968) of *The Atlantic Monthly*, Professor Adam Yarmolinksy, who as Mr. McNamara's chief assistant was in a position to know, tells us how each stage of the escalation in the Vietnam war was decided upon without enthusiasm, and he tells us also something of the inertia of and the unquestioning obedience to outworn axioms that governed so many of the decisions. Perhaps without meaning to do so he advises us once again that one should always in studying the behavior of governments be prepared to acknowledge a good deal of ignorance and perverseness of judgment as well as the influence of emotions.

Moreover, psychological theories do not adjust easily to man's considerable adjustment to the enormous changes in the character of war that have taken place in modern times and especially over the last 25 years. Nuclear weapons have clearly made a critical difference in man's proclivity for war because almost anyone has enough sense to know that they are very dangerous. There are no doubt other factors of comparable influence, including man's experience with two world wars. One notices too that some nations formerly warlike have been pacific for centuries, like Denmark or Sweden, not because of changes either in the genes or in the emotions of the inhabitants but because of changes in the circumstances surrounding those states.

If only enough persons who really were at home in the world of psychoanalysis, which is to say who understook deeply the inner springs of human motivation or compulsion residing in the unconscious, could take the time to study intensively the circumstances pertaining to some historic crises of confrontation and war, we should undoubtedly get some significant insights that are presently denied us. But, as I indicated earlier, the people with the appropriate equipment have to be prepared to acknowledge the existence both of problems and of data of which they are presently ignorant, and to be ready to take the time and make the effort te reduce their ignorance in those spheres. Thus far, it has not happened to any noticeable extent. From the other side, a few historians and political scientists have managed to acquire more than a bowing acquaintance with psychoanalysis, perhaps even through having contributed substantially to the income of one or more analysts. A few even use it effectively in their work. But they are very few, and anyway, in this area the distance between amateur and professional is formidable.

As we turn now to political theories of war causation, we come to what is essentially a melange of notions and ideas which have in common only the fact that they have rarely been thought through. On the utopian side we have the idea of "world government" as a positive cure for the greatest scourge of mankind. The idea makes strange bedfellows. I doubt whether Drs. Edward Teller and Linus Pauling are agreed politically on anything but the necessity of world government.

I have nothing in principle against world government except that I should always want to know exactly what functions are to be governed and by whom. But I see all kinds of evidence in the political behavior of mankind which makes me put an extremely low probability on its being realized within the next century or so — unless, of course, we first have a large-scale thermonuclear war, after which I should expect to see the world hegemony of a single state. This might indeed be a form of world government but hardly in the utopian sense.

One of the things importantly wrong with world government is that no one seems to want it. That is, no one seems to be willing even to begin paying the price for having it. In saying so, I do not mean to imply that they should. There are good reasons as well as bad why people do not want world government, and in my opinion the good reasons easily predominate. The world is full of a multitude of different people, and considering how imperfectly we manage to govern ourselves, I should not like to see any important part of our government put in the hands of peoples who are remote from us in place and understanding and who have very much less of the advantages of education and material well-being that we possess. Reading the debates that go on in the United Nations General Assembly can be a very sobering experience. I am perfectly willing to have in the United Nations a place where some of the so-called emerging nations should have a chance to express their views, and I can even imagine certain special instances where it might do us good if they had a greater influence on our affairs. But in order for a world government to be of any use, we have to think ot the supranational government having, in the net, a very large influence and a persisting one upon its subject peoples or nations.

Actually, there is a good deal of unifying of nations going on in the world, with or without the benefit of formal organization. The borders between the nations of western Europe are certainly not what they once were. I have a deep conviction that these nations have put war between themselves permanently behind them, and if so, that is a great change from the past.

Related to the idea of world government is that which holds nationalism to be invariably a bad and dirty thing. This idea was particularly prevalent before World War II when all wars seemed to be the result of excessive nationalism.

20

During World War II, however, we applauded that nationalism which enabled some nations to organize a resistance against the Nazi invader. In Vietnam today we deplore the weakness of the feeling of nationalism among the people of the south, which is one of the factors which prevents them from unifying around their government. The other major factor is that the only governments they have been able to produce are hardly worth such rallying. The latter condition is actually to some degree a product of the former. Peoples lacking in any kind of real national feeling — which is after all the major unifying influence that produces the largest political entities of our time — are not likely to produce good governments.

There had also been a good deal of talk of how arms races produce wars. I don't doubt that arms races are often an exacerbating influence in an already tense political situation. I suppose the arms races between the Israelis and their Arab enemies have caused anxieties on both sides, but hardly anyone would doubt that the anxieties would already be there anyway and a good deal of hostilities to boot. The same has been true of historical arms races, like the naval race I mentioned earlier between Great Britain and Germany prior to World War I. It is always a nice question whether arms races are more the product of tensions than the cause of them, and historically one sees some mild arms races which were engendered mostly by technological change and which were neither stimulated very much tension nor productive of it. I have in mind, for example, the modest kind of competition in naval building that attended the fantastically rapid changes in naval armaments in the latter part of the 19th century. This kind of competition is very little noted by historians, and properly so, because it had little influence on international politics.

Today, we have to be concerned about arms races with the Soviet Union but mostly, I think, in order to save vast and possible wasteful expenditures rather than to save our lives. The point is highly relevant with respect to the impending development of a huge new antiballistic missile defense. If such a thing goes forward, as I fear it will — especially with the defeat of Mr. Humphrey who was opposed to it and the election of Mr. Nixon who appears to favor it — it will result in the expenditure of vast sums of money without in the net greatly changing the deterrent effect of the missile forces on both sides. I expect it will prove to be what Senator Frank Church has called it: "Potentially the most colossally expensive sieve in history". On the other hand, I should not expect the erection of a ballistic missile defense on both sides to result in any significant deterioration in relations between the Soviet Union and ourselves. Some kinds of arms races actually help greatly to stabilize relations between nations, like the provision of underground silos for both the American and Soviet ballistic missiles, which enormously reduces fears of surprise attack and therefore makes the finger on the nuclear trigger far less itchy than it might otherwise be.

The idea that the development of hostile blocs or alliances can stimulate the outbreak of wars stems very much from the experience of the outbreak of World War I. Certainly the alliance sytems at that time caused what might have been a small and brief war to become a huge, prolonged, and terribly devastating one. On the other hand, alliances are supposed to have some deterrent value too.

Remember Winston Churchill's remark in 1938: "What I see is a bloc on one side and a rabble on the other". I think it important to avoid any special bias for or against alliances but rather to fall back on the conception that wisdom in our foreign policy is always a good thing if we can achieve it, and wisdom is very much needed when it comes to determining what sorts of military commitments abroad we should make or avoid. My own inclination leans towards minimizing such commitments rather than expanding them, mostly because our expansion of such commitments since World War II has been more guided by hothouse axioms than I should like. On the other hand, it is worth remembering that in the two major wars we have been engaged in since World War II, that is Korea and Vietnam, our involvment in each case was not the result of a formal commitment. Maybe there is some lesson in that. With an acknowledged formal commitment there might at least have been some chance of determent. By intervening, despite being free of commitment, we managed to achieve the worst of both worlds.

When we go finally into historical theories of causation, we find ourselves dealing with the alleged explanations of the outbreak of particular wars. I think there are a few general lessons to be derived from some of our experience in attributing certain specific causes to particular wars. I have already referred to the tendency to recast history in terms of some prevailing fashionable philosophy, like the idea that President Wilson projected us into World War I not because of the German resumption of unrestricted submarine warfare but because of his desire to protect investments of certain munitions makers. There are many such examples. The late Charles Beard was supposed to be a respectable historian, yet he found it necessary because of the times he lived in to write a Marxian interpretation of the writing of the United States Constitution. We have also, for at least the last 30 years, been living under the domination of what has been called the "revisionist" school of history concerning the American Civil War. This school considers that war to have been, to quote a book title of one revisionist author, *The Needless War*. No doubt all wars are in a sense needless, but perhaps a war fought over slavery is less needless than most. This school has held the outbreak of the American Civil War to have been due mostly to the fulminations of wild men called abolitionists, rather than those who were at least as emotionally charged in their defense of a peculiar and evil institution.

History is the major tool in teaching us about the relevant behavior of man concerning the outbreak of war and also concerning the relevant changes in man's attitudes and behavior. But it has to be good history, which is to say correct, relevant and perceptive history. Our historians do their best, but they may need some help and encouragement, from time to time, from scholars in other fields. There are, however, very distinguished contemporary historians who scoff at the notion that the other social sciences, including psychoanalysis, might have something to offer them concerning their own art. We also see historians, like scholars in other fields, highly committed to fashionable schools of thought of which nothing is more certain than that they will not last.

Above all, historians have to know what is worth looking for before they can write really relevant history. To give you one example, some two years ago I found myself searching through four different books dealing with the Berlin Blockade of 1948—49 in order to find out just what were the Soviet moves which caused our government to feel that West Germany was being blockaded by force. I did so because I had developed the suspicion that we had not actually been so blockaded. None of the authors had thought it worth while to specify just what those actions were. I wrote to one of them asking if he could inform me by mail. His reply was that it would require additional research, and he inquired whether I would be able to raise the money for him to conduct that research.

I would not be harder on the historians than on my own profession. My intent, I trust, is not to be hard on anyone. I have only been inherently eclectic and comprehensive. That theory, which does not take into account the relevance of all sorts of diverse factors, is bound for that very reason to be wrong. Psychology or psychoanalysis can tell us much, but we have to remember that decisions are made through bodies of men and bureaucracies which go to make up governments or regimes, and that besides having a special mode of operation, these governments or regimes always carry a heavy baggage of notions about their national interests and the like. Similarly, I would put economic causation very low indeed, especially in modern times, but I should also want to remember that differences between great and lesser powers are usually differences in wealth and in the means of making portions of that wealth available for military purposes. In a word, I should be ready to look always for the complexities in the causes of war and to be extremely suspicious of simplistic solutions. When men say that wars are due to innate aggression, my response is that they are using words which tend more to obscure meaning than to clarify it. Aggression and aggressiveness is a common manifestation of mankind, but so are many other relevant factors, like ignorance and stupidity, which as words used by themselves also mean virtually nothing.

If we ever succeed in refining any intellectually acceptable theory of the causation of war, the question will remain whether we will be able to do much about those causes. A generation ago, some political scientists like Professor Quincy Wright, then of the University of Chicago, used to make the distinction between general causes of war and what they called "key" causes. The latter were those causes which were not necessarily the most important but which could be manipulated. For example, the existence of independent nation-states may not be the basic reason for the causation of war, but if we could manipulate the world environment to reduce the autonomy of these states, that is to produce a world government, we would then be dealing with what could be called a key cause. My example is perhaps an unfortunate one. Possibly on the other hand it is just the kind to warn us that proper knowledge is not only hard to come by, but we must not expect too much utility from it in advance. My own nomination for a key instrument would simply be a greater infusion of wisdom into the conduct of our foreign policy, but having said that I am not about to propose nostrums for bringing about that happy state of affairs.

23

Animal Aggression and Its Implications for Human Behavior

HERBERT FRIEDMANN

The fact that a zoologist interested in animal behavior was asked to contribute to a lecture series on "War and the Human Race" suggests that it was thought that aggressive behavior, like an anatomical structure or a physiological process, is something that man shares with the rest of the animal kingdom, no matter how it may have been changed through evolutionary development to its peculiarly human characteristics. It is true that aggression is a very widespread phenomenon in animals of varying degrees of morphological, ethological, and social complexity. If anything, the results of studies of animal behavior in the last few decades have shown more rather than fewer parallels and similarities between animals and man. In the course of this lecture, I shall try to describe the main types of aggressive behavior, limiting myself largely to the "higher" animals, that is to the vertebrates, which are more comparable to man than are the simpler or, at least, what we in our vanity consider to be the "lower" orders. I shall also try to outline how these types of behavior have come to have evolutionary value, how they have been altered or even redirected by natural selection to serve a biologically beneficial role for their possessors.

In keeping with the invitation to discuss with you animal aggression with as much relevance as possible to similar behavior in man, I find that I should state at the outset that it is easier to show that man is still one of the beasts than it is to find clues in the behavioral patterns of his lower relatives that may lend themselves to effective utilization in interpreting, to say nothing of influencing, human aggressiveness, now heralded as precariously on the brink of ushering in what may be a terminal experience.

It is also only proper to state before going further that the studies culminated by recent books and papers by such leading investigators of animal behavior as Konrad Lorenz, Nikko Tinbergen, R.A. Hinde and W.H. Thorpe, among others, and of popularizers and summarizers like Desmond Morris and Robert Ardrey, have served to bring into focus much that was previously disconnected and particularly have brought much of it to the attention of the intelligent, though not necessarily specialized, reading public. That such interpretive summaries could be written, as Lorenz's *On Aggression* Ardrey's *The Territorial Imperative* or Morris's *The Naked Ape*, is evidence that the bits and pieces of recent ethological research are beginning to fit together and to form a meaningful picture. I wish to acknowledge my indebtedness to Lorenz's book and to Tinbergen's 1968 paper in *Science*, in particular, in helping me to sort out and to arrange pertinent topics for this lecture, and for a number of the cases included in this talk.

To turn now to the matter of aggression, we must make it clear that the term is used only to describe hostile or unfriendly behavior between individuals of the same species. It is not aggressive behavior that we observe when we see a predator, such as a lion, attacking and killing a zebra or an antelope. This is merely the way a lion gets its dinner. The lion has no feeling of enmity toward the zebra; the presence of the latter evokes no resentment and arouses no antipathy in the former even though the result could not possibly be worse for it had it done so. I think we would hardly consider the gentle dairy cow aggressive because it eats grass, and there is little difference between its relation to grass and that of the predator to its prey. The cow has an easier time of it and its vegetable food has less chance of escape or of defense.

The popular notion that wild animals, especially those of considerable size and strength, spend most of their time fighting each other is completely wrong. While moving picture makers may film such encounters and then offer the pictures as exciting parts of their scenarios, they fail to state that in almost all such cases the contending beasts have been deliberately pitted against each other in enclosed settings where neither can make an exit when tired of the meaningless fight.

One other point must be made clear. Aggressiveness, like any other behavioral trait, is species characteristic, that is, the degree to which it is called into expression and the mode of that expression, and the intensity and duration of the behavior its release engenders are all as much the special characteristics of each individual species as are its structural form or the pattern of its coloration or the bodily movements with which that form and coloration are used. The biologist, which is tantamount to saying the student of evolution, therefore considers this discrete amount or form of aggression just as much the result of evolution and just as subject to the effective influence of natural selection as any other aspect of the organism. Therefore when studying aggression as an innate part of the totality of the organism the biologist is not only inclined to ask "What is it for" but is compelled to do so if he is to arrive at any understanding of it.

This point, that aggression in each species has forms and dimensions peculiar to that species, and the preceding point, that aggression ordinarily exists only between individuals of the same species, together prepare us for the observation that what directly affects or threatens the existence of an animal species is never the predator that might eat it, but the competitor of its own kind. The old Darwinian concept of the "struggle for existence" is most operative within the population of each species; it has a different meaning and a different set of values of a long-term, rather than a more immediate, nature between species. When we stop to consider that aggressive behavior between individuals of the same kind may work for the good of the species as a whole, as we shall see, we must realize that aggression must be one of the aspects of the species affected by natural selection in its ceaseless and relentless operations.

One further clarification is necessary that we may judge the nature of animal aggression. This has to do with the world in which animals live and act, either aggressively or otherwise. The entire biological world, outside of man, is an amoral one; right and wrong do not exist as ethical values as they do with us. Whatever is good for a species in the long run will act to its advantage in the operation of natural selection; whatever is bad for it will count against it and, if sufficiently critical, may even lead to its extinction. If aggressive behavior were to become developed in one species to the point where it was critically detrimental to the welfare of that animal, the species simply would not survive. The fact that aggression still occurs in a great many kinds of animals which show no signs of dying out or of altering the mode and extent of their aggression, in itself should inform us that this type of behavior, kept within proper limits, is not harmful to the animals that exhibit it.

The whole biological world is populated with countless hundreds of thousands of kinds of organisms, and the only reason that they exist, rather than those others that have had their day or that have failed in the long history of life, is that they are more able in their present environmental circumstances to reproduce and to pass on to their successors their own particular combination of hereditary characters. If they did not do this they would disappear. During the enormous time span of evolution countless millions of little alterations, increments to, or diminutions of, specific traits have appeared, but only those that were passed on to succeeding generations can possibly have played a part in further evolutionary change. An uninherited character dies with the individual that possesses it. Since evolution depends on the transmission of slowly developed changes through the germ plasm from each generation to the next one, it becomes obvious that the primary test of adequacy for living in this amoral world and for succeeding in it, as evidenced by increase of its population and of the extent of the available environment occupied by a given species, is the extent to which the genetic characters of each of its component individuals are contributed to the gene pool of their immediate successors.

This means that aggressive behavior, as one of the characteristics of a species, can only have evolved to its particular mode or dimension because its presence helped the survival, through reproduction, of the summation of the increments that many generations successively contributed to create its present aspect, and this, in turn, tells us that it must have met with the impassive approval of natural selection, that uncompromising, amoral judge of fitness. In other words, it tells us that the various forms and degrees of aggression found today in different species must be of some use to them, certainly not detrimental to them.

It is particularly important that we realize this when we attempt to pass from a consideration of animals to that of man. This is so because in man we have a creature that has created a rapidly changing environment of his own, what we call his culture, and this in turn has come to affect his behavior patterns more and more with the result that they are no longer merely subject to natural selection. Because intra-specific aggression in the human race has gotten out of hand and has become a most serious threat to the survival of the species, we naturally, and rightly, condemn such aggression as something basically evil, something to be controlled if not eradicated. This, however, does not justify us in assuming that in other animals aggression must, of necessity, be equally bad.

There are two general modes of vertebrate animal existence, the solitary, or at most a pair or family during the reproductive season, and the gregarious or colonial way of living. In those vertebrates that do not form colonies, herds, flocks, or other groupings of varying degrees of social structure, we find that aggression serves three main functions: it effects a balanced distribution of the individuals of a species over the available environment; it contributes toward the selection of the strongest individuals through the competitive process of rival fights, thereby ensuring the optimal parents for the next generation; and it contributes to the survival of the young through their more adequate defense by stronger parents. We may now take these three in turn.

Many animals live in loose, practically unorganized aggregations of varying degrees of density during the winter or the nonbreeding season but become solitary with the advent of spring. This has been studied more extensively and intensively in many kinds of birds than in other creatures, and in the case of birds it is usually the male that establishes what is now generally known as an individual breeding territory. The size of the territory varies with the species but is usually related to the food productivity required to satisfy the needs of the male, his mate and the future offspring of the season. The male is rigidly bound to the limits of his territory and is very aggressive toward any other male of his own kind that encroaches upon his domain. It sometimes happens that a second male may be stronger and may succeed in driving out the first one, but generally the owner of a territory exhibits a greater intensity of aggression than does an invader. The actual fighting between two birds is done largely with the wings and the feet, and while the battle may be intense and of several minutes or more in duration it seldom results in the death of either participant. The loser usually gives up and leaves. The territory owner may pursue the would-be invader beyond the limits of the territory, but its aggression diminishes sharply once outside its own domain. If anything, the defender may suddenly act as if it were almost frightened by its own courage, whereupon it quickly flies back ito its "home base" where it seems to feel safe and is once more ready to attack the intruder should the latter attempt a re-entry.

The renewed strength or courage that the bird derives from being on its territory is reminiscent of the story in Greek mythology of Antaeus. This hero, we may remember, was a giant in Libya who challenged all strangers traversing his country to a wrestling bout. As he derived renewed strength and courage whenever he touched his native soil, whether with his feet if he were doing well in the match, or with any other part of his body if he were thrown by his adversary, he proved invincible and acquired great renown. He was finally beaten by Hercules, who learning the secret of his strength, held him up off the ground and crushed him in his mighty arms.

But usually the intruding bird is no Hercules and the local feathered Antaeus wins out. Later when the territory owner attracts and acquires a mate for the season, the hen may also participate in the defense of the territory, although by then the unestablished males have generally dispersed farther afield where they, in turn, have found suitable areas and have set up their own territories.

27

The function of territory is the spacing of the members of the species so that there will be enough food for all and for their broods. This obviation of the danger of too dense a population of an animal species in one part of the available environment, thereby exhausting its food resources and then starving, is the most important survival value of intra-specific aggression. While aggressive behavior in territorial defense makes this possible, there has, at the same time, been evolved a way of diminishing fighting, of saving the energy and time spent in aggressive behavior. This is the evolution of song in birds. When a male has become established in a territory he chooses a favorite perch, usually on a conspicuous branch, from which he repeats his song. It is now generally agreed among ethologists that while the song serves as an inducement to the females seeking mates, it also acts as a warning to other males telling them, in effect, that here is a male established on a territory and that they better not intrude. The observational evidence suggests that it is effective in reducing the frequency of territorial combat. The degrees of loudness, carrying power and tonal suggestions available in the range of variation in the song of a given kind of bird, have been acted on over the ages by natural selection, and their selective value has apparently been measured with respect to both functions — mate attraction and competitor discouragement. What a wonderful way to reduce the opportunity for aggression and what a pity it is not applicable to man.

In a different way some mammals, such as rats and dogs not equipped with song, mark the limits of their territories by urinating or defecating at peripheral spots thereby leaving a series of olfactory notices to others of their kind that this is their domain and that entry into it will be opposed. These mammals rely on their sense of smell as a final test, they have been said to "think through their noses", and they are quick to pick up, even to look for these olfactory evidences of the safety or the peril of going into a given place.

The second function of aggression is to help in the selection of the strongest individuals by rival fights, particularly with respect to mating rivalries, thereby ensuring the strongest, healthiest, optimal male parents for the next generation. Here we must realize as Darwin long ago pointed out that it is always to the advantage, it is always favorable to the future of a species if the stronger, the more powerful of two rival males takes possession of the desired female. This, together with territorial spacing of the males, has the effect of allowing the weaker individuals to reproduce as well as the others, provided there are enough females to go around. It gives precedence to the stronger but it does not eliminate the weaker. In these rival fights there seldom is an outcome fatal to the loser. One thinks of such things as the rivalry between bull elks where the two may lock their horns in battle and push at each other in this way. It is true that often one finds the skulls of two such combatants whose antlers had become inextricably locked and thereby interfered with normal feeding or living and hastened the death of both. However, this is the exception, not the rule; the permanent locking of antlers happens in only an extremely small percent of all such fights. Even here, we should remember that elk and other deer do not use their horns for fighting predatory enemies; then they use their hoofs, and to a lesser extent, their teeth. In other words, in these mating fights there is an element of "showing off", not of lethal combat, as these contests are often held in the presence of the female.

This brings us to the fact that in many animals the aggressive element in mating rivalries has become redirected by natural selection into what we term courtship displays. In effect, what transpires in these behaviorally ritualized antics is that the male (usually) goes through movements that display most openly and clearly its brightly colored parts, precisely those parts that, as easily recognized marks of specific indentity, ordinarily invite aggression from other males of their kind. These may be specialized, often seasonal, feathers in many birds, multicolored noses and rumps in terrestrial apes such as drills and mandrills, with arrays of pastel purples, pinks, and pale blues that find a parallel in current psychedelic designs, or such otherwise useless but conspicuous growths as the antlers of deer, and brilliantly colored, often erectile, fins of coral reef fishes. Just as the development of song in many kinds of birds has had the effect of reducing the incidence of territorial aggression, so too the ritualization of mating behavior has redirected much aggression into harmless, but effective, competitive courtship display. This is particularly the case in birds, less so in mammals, and other terrestrial vertebrates.

The picture here is not entirely one-sided. Actually, as in the case of coral reef fishes, the fact that many species of similar size and habit live close together, but are all strikingly different in their vivid coloration, serves not to reduce aggressive fighting but to ensure that such aggression be directed chiefly, if not wholly, to individuals of the same species. However, this has the eventual, long-range effect of spacing the individuals, of preventing too many from competing for local food supply or breeding sites, so the result is still for the good of each kind. By and large it appears that aggression has become, through the slow but incessant operation of natural selection, considerably redirected into effective but harmless, competitive, ritualized displays, or reduced in frequency by the warning effect of song in birds or by the leaving of olfactory notices in some mammals. This does not mean that fighting is done away with; it merely means that the frequency with which such aggressive behavior is released is much diminished.

The third function of aggression is that of protecting the relatively or absolutely defenseless young by their parents. Here the degree to which the parents are able to evoke a show of defensive aggression by which they may intimidate and repulse predators is probably proportional to the degree to which mating rivalries help to assure that the strongest and healthiest individuals become the parents rather than the weaker and less effective ones. Also it must be stressed that pugnacious or courageous behavior in defense of the young from the attacks or potential attacks of enemies that would feed on them is different from aggression as we have tried to define it. It is no longer intra-specific since the would-be attackers are usually not individuals of the same species. Nevertheless it merits mention in a discussion of aggression because it makes use of, it is built out of the same elements of behavior that comprise the methods by which aggressive behavior achieves expression.

So far we have discussed the forms and uses of aggression in solitary, nongregarious or colonial animals. It is important to survey the situation in these other creatures as well, particularly since the human species, the special case we must keep in mind for possible comparison, is essentially a social, nonsolitary living creature. Here again, in order to cover the ground without too long a description, without taking the time to discuss variations and details, we may divide the social organization of vertebrate animals into three main types. It hardly need be said that no vertebrate animals exhibit anything comparable to the amazingly complex but seemingly rigidly formalized colonies that we find in social insects such as some ants and bees and termites.

Of the three types of vertebrate aggregations, the simplest may be termed the anonymous flock, a mere aggregation of anonymous members with no individual or "personal" recognition of, or ties to, other equally anonymous members. Such aggregations have been described in invertebrate animals, such as cuttlefish, squids and insects, and in vertebrates as well as in schools of fish, herds of grazing mammals such as bison or antelopes, vast migratory masses of lemmings, blindly driven even to self-destruction, or flocks of ducks or blackbirds or starlings. It is a mistake to assume that these are mere opportunistic assemblages as are the gathering of scavengers around a carcass; they seem to be based on the fact that the individuals of these gragarious species are attracted to, and held together by, the presence of others of their own kind. They would rather be together than apart, and in many cases they would rather be with their own kind than in mixed flocks.

In assemblages of this sort there is little aggression within the flock. This may be a result of the anonymity of each of its members to the others, or it may be that only species with a low aggression-index form such groups. However, in the face of danger there may be a group reaction. Lorenz has written that he could not name a single gregarious animal species whose individuals do not press together when alarmed by the onset of a predator. What we find in these anonymous flocks is not so much aggressive behavior as a common reaction to danger from without. There is a safety in numbers; predators usually do not attack a large herd but wait for one individual to become separated from it; birds of prey seem to become somewhat bewildered by too many smaller birds at once, which impairs their ability to settle on and to aim at a particular one.

The fact that many species tend to form anonymous flocks would seem directly opposed to the spacing or dispersing effect of intra-specific aggression. It is true these are contrary forces but the resulting situation does not always rule out less extreme manifestations of the two conflicting drives. This is true in colonial nesting birds where each pair still has and defends its own nest, which, by the exigencies of crowding in a large colony, is practically coterminous with its individual territory. In most of these species, such as sea birds nesting on cliffs, or swallows under the eaves, there can, of necessity, be no spatial relation of the nesting area to the feeding grounds, the open ocean in the former or the insect laden sky in the latter case. Another type of manifestation is revealed in what has been termed "individual distance" maintained between starlings on a telegraph wire, where the distance is exactly that at which two starlings can reach each other with their beaks. Yet, on the whole, anonymously gregarious species lack aggressive tendencies. Because of this and because of the very anonymity of its members we may consider the anonymous flock to have little relevance to human behavior. Yet, in times of mass panic, such as a fire in a theatre, humans act with equally little regard for each other, with equal anonymity, and with a mass blindness not dissimilar to the onward surging of hordes of lemmings or of stampeding buffaloes. It was to overcome this innate tendency that steamship lines deliberately encouraged the slogan of "women and children first" in case of salvage in the event of maritime disaster, and dunned this into the minds of men so that it too achieved some degree of innate spontaneity. It may be that the human species has evolved a long way from the simplest form of aggregation, the anonymous flock, but in times of acute distress his reversion to it suggests that it still lingers in his psychobiological background.

The second type of social organization in vertebrates may be termed the collective community, of which the best known, most completely studied example is that of the European brown rat. Here, in distinction from the anonymous flock, the group arises from one family, the merging of generations of one closely knit group. However, in spite of this mode of origin the members of the community, or clan, show little direct evidence of individual recognition of, or of feelings toward, other individuals in the group. There is little aggressive or other incompatible behavior between them; the whole community seems peaceful and orderly, but the whole group have a tremendous aggression, seemingly always ready to be released, against any rat of another community. Apparently the rats of each community have a common odor by which they recognize each other, just as seems to be the case in some of the social insects. Within each community or, to take another example, within each wolf pack, there is no real fighting, at least not more than slight friction as might be expected in crowded quarters. Intra-community or intra-family fights are rare and occur only when a stranger, a rat from another community happens to have entered the scene. This arouses such intense aggression that the reaction seems to spill over between fellow-members of the community or clan. What rats do when a member of an alien rat community enters their domain or is put there by a human experimenter is one of the most horrible and utterly vicious things known in any animals. The stranger may run around for some minutes until it comes close enough for one of the local rats to notice its alien smell. This information seems to pass instantaneously throughout the group, all of whose members, in a state of great excitement, with their hair raised on end and their eyes bulging, set out to find and to kill the intruder. In their excitement, if two of them collide they bite each other and may go on fighting until they sniff each other, whereupon they part peacefully. The strange rat, if not rescued or removed by the experimenter, is literally torn to pieces by the resident ones.
experimenter, is literally torn to pieces by the resident ones.

We ask what is the biological purpose of this intense group hate between rat clans. It is an extreme case of intensity of aggression, and so far we have no real, proved understanding of its function. It would seem, that given this tendency to aggression,the intermittent, or even more frequent, warfare between neighboring families or communities of rats would exert great selection pressure

31

in favor of pugnacity and strength and would place the smaller group at a disadvantage, as all the rats of each clan help each other in the inter-clan battle. The only thing that may be suggested is that rats are creatures with great aggressiveness and with ferocious behavior tendencies and can stand the inhibitions of a social organization less readily than can gentler creatures, and that consequently the pent-up aggression, unexpendable under ordinary circumstances, literally pours forth at every opportunity such as that provided by the advent of an alien, though very similar, rat. It is possible that this intensity of aggression has thus not proved harmful to the rat as a species, and that the pressure of natural selection acts on the community as a unit as well as on each individual as a member of the clan. Furthermore, the ever present tendency to aggression, kept in a state of passivity, like that of any other innate behavior pattern, suffers a marked lowering of the threshold value of the stimuli needed to elicit it. The fact is that aggression is inhibited only within the group, not between neighboring groups, and it may well have a spacing value between groups, somewhat similar to that of territory among individuals of other solitary species. It may be asked why has not aggression been done away with in the course of evolution, since it may seem more detrimental to the everyday life of animals than beneficial. The answer is that it still is beneficial in the ways already pointed out — spacing of individuals or colonies so as not to outstrip the local food supply, ensuring the best and healthiest individuals as the progenitors of the next generation, and improving the defense of that generation while too young to take care of itself.

Cynics, at times, have likened the human species to the rat, and have claimed that no good can be expected of either. Cynicism, however, depends for its formulation on willful selection of the evidence to be used and willful rejection of the evidence to be discarded or ignored. If, at times, human communities — families, villages, or even larger aggregates — may act as badly as rats, yet there are many basic differences which completely upset the contrived conclusions of the cynics and which we hardly need to go into here.

We may now get a pleasanter picture of animal behavior and of the role of aggression in it, by turning to the third type of social organization, which we may term the inter-cognizant or non anonymous flock. The best known, most completely documented cases of these happen to be of bird species such as the jackdaw, a European crow, and the greylag goose. I should mention that what we find in these is also found in many other species. These are essentially groups of families in which individual bonds or ties to fellow members on a personalized, individualized basis are present. In the rat clan there is nothing to suggest that each member knows the other except by their similarity of odor; in these birds the mates know each other, they act as if they miss each other when one is absent; the parents know their offspring even after they have fledged and left the nest, and the offspring know their parents.

Within the colony of jackdaws, of geese, of domestic chickens, a certain amount of aggression takes place, but it is of a relatively mild and somewhat redirected form. The encounters are brief but decisive; the victor from then on is in a superior social position to the loser, and usually it is the older members of the group that are "on top". This resulting social ranking is known as the "peck order", because it was first studied in flocks of domestic chickens. In effect it means that a high-ranking individual may peck at an individual of lower rank, without the latter attempting to peck back. In a short time the members of a small flock become arranged in a definite peck order. As a result there develops a firmness of social structure beneficial to the smooth working of the whole group. This is true also in jackdaws, and in them, as well as in other species, we find that the established firmness of social organization reveals itself in a remarkable way. Whenever two lower-ranking individuals begin fighting, as is almost impossible to avoid entirely in a compact social group, the high-ranking birds react to the stimulus of visible aggression by taking part, and they always interfere on the side of the weaker or the losing party. This is not in any sense a moral intervention but is actuated by the fact that the stronger of the fighting pair evinces greater aggression and thereby arouses greater aggressive response from the interferers. While this undoubtedly acts as a device for causing the cessation of aggression, it has the effect of protecting the weaker individual, a form of social welfare that it took mankind some time to formulate in his own social structure.

As an example of the social status or influence of the high-ranking, usually the older, individuals in such a group of animals we may take a case involving chimpanzees studied by Yerkes. The chimpanzee is an animal capable of learning by imitation, which points up very clearly the following observation. Yerkes took one of the younger, low-ranking chimps from the group, put it in a separate enclosure and there taught it to remove bananas from a specially designed feeding apparatus that involved complicated manipulation on its part. When this ape was brought back to the group and the feeding apparatus was installed there, it immediately repeated what it had learned and continued to do so to its own advantage. None of the other chimps showed any interest or even watched it. Then Yerkes did the same identical thing with the top-ranking member of the group and found when it was similarly returned to its fellows they all watched it and soon learned to imitate it and to get their bananas in this way.

The biological value of rank or status within a group is essentially that the whole company benefits from the experience, from what we might call, in quotes, the wisdom of its older members, roughly comparable to what humans do when they follow the guidance or actions of those of their group whose status inspires their respect.

One last, but by no means least, item should be mentioned. We have already said that in geese, in chickens, in jackdaws, and chimpanzees, there is a "personal" bond between individuals. In the case of mates, and some of these matings, as in geese, last for the lifetime of the pair, i.e. until the death of the first one to die, which may mean as long a period as 40 years in some cases, it is important to realize that the formation of such a durable emotional bond is in itself, to some degree, a redirected form of aggression.

In the simultaneous complex of innate drives, what Lorenz calls the great parliament of instincts, the main drives, sexuality, escape, and aggression, go through mutual adjustments as needed. Thus in Cichlids, little fishes commonly kept in aquaria and much and carefully studied by ethologists, the ratio of mixtures of these drives is different in the two sexes. If the male has even the slightest fear of his would-be partner, his sexuality does not find expression, apparently does not even try to evince itself; if the female is not so completely unafraid of her potential mate that all her aggressive behavior is wholly suppressed, if not extinguished, she does not react to him sexually at all. If she has not attained this state of total nonaggression the female responds in the opposite way and attacks the male, and the intensity of this attack is directly correlated with her readiness for sexual response. It is almost as though sex and aggression are merely aspects of the same innate drive and are aspects that do not merge but must replace each other. If the female's aggression is wholly suppressed she may still flee from the male rather than accept him, but then she takes advantage of every pause or twist or turn or other opportunity in her retreat to perform sexually motivated courtship movements. It makes one think of the unconscious accuracy of the old cartoonist who drew two hens running from a rooster, and one of them saying to the other "Maybe we're running too fast".

In the greylag goose studied so well and so long by Lorenz, the onset of the mating bond is marked by individual aggression. As long as the female is still the least bit aggressive to the male she will not permit him to mount her; the male, on the contrary, is unable to mate unless his aggression in maintained unimpaired, so the two go through what may be a prolonged, often an interrupted, series of meetings until the aggression level or quotient of each is simultaneously at the right stage. Then, and not until then, is mating achieved.

The ritualized courtship behavior is, as we have already mentioned, to a considerable degree a redirected form of aggression. What transpires in the consummation of courtship into mating is that each of the prospective mates comes to sense that the aggression of the other is for outsiders only, and not directed against itself. Once mated, the bond between them is constant and the question of mutual aggression no longer arises. This is one of the most incredible turnabouts imaginable. The personal bond, the individual-to-individual friendship, is found only in creatures with highly developed intra-specific aggression, and it is more lasting, more soundly established, the more aggressive the particular species may be. The duration of the pair bond in species of more limited aggressiveness, such as many kinds of small song birds, is limited to a single season, and in some cases, to a single brood even if two or more broods may be reared in the one year. Of course, these birds have a much shorter life span than the geese we have been discussing. The tie, the pair bond, whether permanent or annual, is in effect the ideal solution; each member may still be aggressive toward others of its sex, but their mutual aggressiveness is completely buried, if not actually eliminated.

We have seen by now that in animals aggression is kept within bounds, or is redirected to useful purposes, indeed even to purposes quite the opposite of hostility — to pair formation, individual friendship and durable amity. It is not impossible that individual friendship may have been evolved as a method of bringing to a halt the aggression of the two individuals toward each other in order to enable them to fight other individuals more effectively. In its origins it may have been just as cold-blooded as that. As a matter of fact, even without troubling to review the ramifications of the role, the expression, and the transformation of aggression, we could have predicted that in a biological world constantly under the surveillance of natural selection, uncontrolled and harmful aggression would have doomed its perpetrators to extinction.

We may now ask what, if anything, has our knowledge of aggression in animals to give us that may be useful in our attempt to control and to curb it in humans. Man is no exception to the animal world, he has innate aggressive tendencies, and this we must recognize. If we were dealing solely with biological man, with man as an animal, we could point out that redirection of aggression might be of great help. We find this today in the wide-spread interest in sports, even in highly organized, professional sports because there the spectators who so vastly outnumber the players seem to identify themselves with the teams they favor, and to that extent experience a vicarious release of otherwise pent-up aggression. So effective in satisfying the aggressive tendencies are these organized sports exhibitions, that Lorenz was moved to observe that the Olympic Games were about the only event at which the playing of the national anthems of the competing teams aroused no antipathies among the multinational conglomeration of spectators.

But surely games and athletic contests are not going to solve the human dilemma. The reason is that in the case of man we are dealing with a creature that has become the product not only of biological evolution but also of cultural evolution. In the present crisis of human affairs the results of his own cultural evolution have come to outweigh those of the past development that he shares with the rest of creation. Physically and genetically, man has changed but little for thousands of years so far as we know, but culturally he has changed enormously and is constantly and rapidly changing.

In comparing man to the rest of the animal kingdom, we should keep in mind that there is a very significant difference in the mode of expression of the habits of the two. In animals a particular habit may have a definite biological end, may serve a useful purpose for the species, but there is no reason for supposing that the individual animal exhibiting the habit has any thought or knowledge of why it is doing what it does. Merely fulfilling the routine expression of the action required by the habit satisfies the individual even if the biological end is not attained in every case. In man, on the contrary, the individual does have some understanding of the reason for, or the advantage of, a particular behavior pattern. It is because of this ability to judge the value and the outcome of his actions that civilized man has come to consider as virtues such unnatural concepts as industriousness and thrift, and even to raise them to the moral level of honor and honesty. The fact that man, alone among animals, can anticipate and can and does worry about the future results of what he does, not only differentiates him from the animals but gives reason for thinking that his actions will be less blindly innate and immutable than those of animals. We must keep this in mind in comparing aggression in the two.

In man we are not dealing with unaided individual aggression, where the behavior might be realized with fists, feet, and teeth, but with dehumanized, mechanized, weaponry-assisted aggression, where a mild-mannered, even kindly or timid, individual may release from far-away a bomb aimed at a village to the inhabitants of which he has no personal animosity. Soldiers, who, as civilized human beings, would shrink from shooting and burning innocent civilians, women and children, become mere pawns in the military machine, and may even derive some feeling of satisfaction and pride from the accuracy of their marksmanship. This kind of situation does not occur in any of the animals; it is a peculiarly human extension of aggressive behavior far beyond its usual accompaniment of physical or mental emotional state. Also, where in animals, intra-specific fighting is seldom to the death but usually terminates when the loser runs away, in man's artificially constructed concept of warfare, running away is considered cowardly or shameful even though it may be biologically the sensible thing for the individual to do. It is only when the commanding officers decide the battle is lost, that running away is justified by terming it a strategical retreat. This is not intended as a criticism of military behavior judgments; it is intended only to point out the great difference between them and those involved in animal aggression. It may be argued if warfare is really comparable to animal aggression, as it is not necessarily accompanied originally by anger and by physical excitement and exertion as far as each participant is concerned. It might be added that the "hard bargaining" that goes on daily as a routine part of business, between individual humans and between nations as well, is similar to aggression — a form of aggression held within recognized legal limits — and that this may be a cultural restriction of man's aggressive attitudes just as we have found animal aggression sometimes rendered harmless to individuals by ritualization into courtship displays.

Allowing for a residual amount of aggression and territoriality in the human species, the biologist would be apt to point out that probably the surest way to arouse this latent aggression, as in other vertebrates, would be to infringe upon man's concept of group territory. Where in animals such trespassing will result in a fight to a decision, leaving only the winner in the area of combat, in man the intellectual understanding of the superiority in armed or economic or political power of the invader may force the invaded to accept defeat but still to remain where he was, to repress his aggression because the battle seems hopeless. This does not mean that the aggression is done away with. It is merely hidden, biding its time; the feeling of group territory and of a desire to defend it persists even in the face of the most unlikely and unpropitious circumstances.

In man, territory is a group, rather than an individual, concern, more like that of the collective community as described in the brown rat earlier in this lecture. Also in man, the more civilized the group or society, the greater is the tendency to substitute group territory for individual ones. The influx of people from the rural areas, characterized by obvious, visible territories, such as small farms, to the cities devoid of such individual land holdings, devoid of relatively self-sufficient units, strongly suggests that in cultural man, as contrasted with the hypothecated biological man, the things that gregarious living has to offer outweigh whatever force the old vestiges of individual territorialism may still

36

have. This is true not only of civilized urban man but also of such relatively simple social groups as the pygmies of the Congo forests, the bushmen of the Kahalari, and the eskimos of the arctic tundra.

In the case of civilized man a further complication must be kept in mind. Intra-specific aggression in animals is always between similar individuals, individuals with the same habits and the same needs. In urbanized man the picture is different: there are vast discrepancies in knowledge, in habits, in education, in tastes, in desires, in accepted modes of thinking and of evaluating, in religious and political mental modes or barriers among individuals and even more so among larger groups. There is, consequently, less complete mutual identification between contesting individuals than in animals, and this affects the nature of the aggression between them.

I cannot help but think that part of the present widespread interest in aggression is based on the assumption that there is no real difference between two animals fighting and man's potential use of atomic weapons against others of his own species, with the very real danger of world-wide disaster. While this assumption seems to me far-fetched as far as behavioral biology is concerned, there is enough of a residual problem to warrant our attempt to compare the peculiarly human maladjustment with the total picture of animal aggression.

A knowledge of the various methods by which aggression has been controlled or redirected in the biological world may offer some information relative to the human situation, but by itself it is not likely to be very effective as a guide. It is necessary that we should think of redirection of innate aggression in terms of the cultural more than the biological part of man. Not only does biological man, like the rest of animal creation, have within him a latent tendency for intra-specific aggression, but this may burst forth so rapidly and so easily on such relatively slight stimulation, that we must never forget its presence, dormant though it be at times, and we must be prepared for its sudden and unfortunate manifestations.

The population explosion, and on top of this, the flow of people from rural to the already cumbersomely large and crowded urban areas seems almost designed to proliferate occasions for irritation and aggression. As we have seen in some animals the innate drive for aggression under conditions of crowding finds expression with lower thresholds of stimuli than in better spaced, roomier arrangements. Not only is this true in man, but in his case the rapidity of travel and of communication tends to bring together divergent and often not completely compatible groups or nations, and this too increases the opportunities for mutual displeasure and misunderstanding, and for possible hostility.

There is a great difference between the spatial and temporal immediacy of the stimulus and the aggression it releases in animals, and a war such as that in Vietnam where our involvement stems from a political-idealogical attitude concerning an area far from our own territorial commitment. In civilized man the concept of territory has assumed ideational limits so far beyond actual physical or geographical perimeters that to consider it in the same sense as territoriality in animals stretches the concept to the point where its useful definition breaks down. It is possible that this psycho-biologically unreal aspect

37

of the situation is one of the things that affects our feelings and helps to create a vast impatience in us when the Vietnam war is discussed.

It must be apparent by now that I consider the nature of aggression in animals sufficiently different from the mechanized war habits developed by man to permit ready translation from one to the other. Man's mushrooming scientific and technological progress, coupled with his ability, unparalleled in the animal kingdom, to pass on his learning and his skills, through the peculiarly human development of language and symbol, both oral and written, has enabled him to upset and to alter his environment, and to direct to a large extent, his own future evolution. It is not his innate aggression, as such, but his increasing use of energy and power from outside himself that has made it possible for man to bring himself, as many think, to the very rim of total disaster.

One thing that gives reason for some optimism is that the data and the concepts of behavioral biology, of animal ethology, and those of human psychology, particularly the outgrowths of the analytic approach to human behavior, have become increasingly merged into a more unified and more meaningful whole. Where a score of years ago the animal psychologist and the human psychologist or psychiatrist were unable to meet and to discuss their problems and their fields with any mutual advantage, today there is a rapport of understanding that should yield a vast insight that simply did not exist before. This new source of self-knowledge should be of great value in dealing with man's behavioral problems.

At the same time we must be cautious about using the data from animals in interpreting the actions of humans. Thus, as Ardrey has mentioned, one English psychiatrist has already suggested that the space race may be a ritualization of the cold war between America and the Soviet Union, in a way comparable to that in which in some animals aggression has been ritualized and redirected in competitive courtship antics.

I doubt that it is factual to interpret the space race simply as a redirection or a ritualization of the cold war, because humans, unlike animals, have some idea of why they do what they do and would therefore not be so easily sidetracked. It is our misfortune that in the biological prehistory of mankind natural selection apparently had no need for placing a premium on behavioral mechanisms, ritualizations or not, that would prevent killing of others of the same species. It was not until the invention of artificial weapons that the balance between lethal aggression and social inhibitions was upset in man. We have seen that in animals, aggression has been constrained, has been redirected, has been ritualized in various ways in different groups and situations. If man were subject solely to the same external selective pressures as are the rest of his fellow creatures, we would have no more chance than they to choose our future course. But we do have the chance; our understanding and our ability to reason with some degree of objectivity should enable us to avert the chaotic calamity that some prophets of doom claim to see. War is not merely aggression on a grand scale, and even though aggressive behavior is part of our animal inheritance, war is not an instinctive, ineradicable or uncontrollable proclivity of the human race. The need for distinguishing between the characteristically animal and the characteristically human aspects of behavior was properly stressed in a recent, closely reasoned lecture at the University of Oxford on *War and Peace in Animals and Man* by Tinbergen. He ended his discourse on the unfortunately pessimistic and defeatist note that even if it is too late to prevent disaster, man should go on studying and learning all he can, a sort of "going down with colors flying" attitude. I think we may find reason for being more optimistic. What man must do is to realize that in his case, unique among all living creatures, he must replace the amoral force of natural selection or, at least, add to it that of moral or ethical selection which is, after all, man's proudest product and his own possible salvation.

Ritual and Intergroup Murder:
Comments on War, Primitive and Modern

JOHN G. KENNEDY

The persistent recurrence of wars in human history has led to a deep-seated and widespread fatalism. Politicians and common people seem to concur that war is an inevitable response to principles of "human nature". This is evident in the self-fulfilling doomed ways they behave, in spite of unceasing platitudes expressing hopes for "peace in the world". Anthropologists unaccountably have not devoted the attention to this overwhelmingly important topic which it merits, and when they have, they have often added their voices to the general fatalism. There are at least two current positions in social science which tend to justify such pessimism. These are the assertions that *man is basically and innately aggressive, and that wars are functionally useful to bring about changes in rigidified societies.*

The idea that man is innately aggressive and that this is the basic cause of wars has a long history, but in this century it has been championed most strongly by psychoanalysis. Lately, however, the idea has found additional support among some ethologists and has again diffused to the public through various popular books and articles (Lorenz, Ardrey, *etc.*). It is not my intention to get into a detailed critique of such work here, but I want to stress that these translations of animal behavior findings to the human level are analogies and *only* analogies. Such arguments tend to fail because the authors do not recognize the complexities of the variables involved, and because they do not give sufficient weight to the tremendous difference which symbolic communication and its consequent, culture, have made on the behavior of the human animal.

I take it as axiomatic that man is characterized by some kind of inherent and biologically based activity drive, and that under conditions of frustration, desire, or fear, this drive is often expressed in the violent behavior which we label aggression. Aggression is also obviously correlated with, and an integral aspect of war, but the relationships between war and aggression are reciprocal, complex, and mediated by intervening variables. There is no simple cause and effect relationship, and as Leslie White (1949, p. 143) and others have long contended, there is probably more evidence to support the proposition that war *produces* aggression than the reverse.

However, my point here is that the arguments from animal behavior, which are alleged to tell us something about the causes of human warfare, are generally inadequate and misleading. It is embarassingly obvious, but apparently necessary to point out, that animals do not wage war at all. As members of species they do not engage in deliberate, organized killing of members of other groups of their own species. Animals do not organize armies to exterminate enemy groups, to take slaves, or to set up kingdoms. More significantly, an animal cannot be taught to hate a specific outgroup enemy of his own species on the basis of past injustices to his identity group. He may be conditioned to respond aggressively to certain cues, but he cannot nurse a desire for revenge.

I am referring here to two special interrelated attributes of Man; his *cumulative culture*, which he passes down from generation to generation, and his *ego*, or self-concept, both of which are founded upon his symbolically derived abilities to remember, communicate, and view himself as an object. The uniquely human ego, so precariously dependent upon symbolic feed-back from its supporting environing group, devoted so largely to avoiding shame and humiliation and to making itself acceptable, makes possible the uniquely *human* forms of aggression. To hate is human, and so is the desire to seek revenge. Shame and guilt, the propensity and ability to extend one's identity to a group, victorious gloating, firing squads, and persistent slaughter of enemies long after the original reasons for dispute have been forgotten, are all characteristics peculiar to Homo Sapiens. The great variances in hostile actions between societies of the world suggest that human aggression is predominantly a *learned* phenomenon. It is elicited by situations and behaviors which are themselves usually manifestations of culture patterns.

The basic difference between the aggressive acts of men and those of other animals may be emphasized by stating that animals kill, but men *murder*. The symbolically socialized human self feels a remorse that no selfless jungle predator feels when it kills another animal. It is the meaning of the act to the actor that counts, not its form. One of my basic contentions here is that *all intentional killing of other men by men is murder*, and that all but the most defectively socialized of men unconsciously know and feel this, and can eventually recognize it consciously. Only by recognizing it, in fact, can war ever be stopped.

Another line of social science thinking that in some of its forms perpetuates the assumption of the inevitability of war is called *functionalism*. From the 19th century evolutionists, notions of the role of warfare in the evolution of the State as a superordinate institution bringing order to ever wider territories and population, came the later notion of the "cultural productivity" of war. For example, Bronislaw Malinowski, a founder of modern functionalist thought, spoke of wars of nationalism as being "culturally productive" because of their role in producing nation-states (1968, p. 258).

The idea of the cultural productivity of war is of course familiar to us all, and is an argument often used by militarists. A recent revival of the notion has been made by the anthropologist Dr. Anthony Leeds (1963). He argues that warfare has positive "adaptive" functions for societies. He considers that war as an "Institution" has such functions as consolidation and centralization of internal power, consolidation of existing trends (such as towards industrialization or centralization), abrogation of "peace rules" (allowing a break with the past), elicitation of innovation in technology and institutions, redefinition of ossified or frozen rules of peace, (he says that normal processes of change may be too slow), and reallocation of resources (presumably through acquisition of territory, cultural diffusion, *etc.*).

41

Such reasoning has a certain persuasiveness, and there is no argument that some such effects have been produced by wars of the past. But the implicit assumption in most such functional interpretations is that there is a kind of positive *requiredness* about war because underlying "needs" must be met. There is also the assumption that past effects of wars must always be repeated in future conflicts. Many of these "functions" imply the "culture lag" assumption that societies become "ossified", the notion that wars only occur because of systematic blockages of people's wants, and that results are therefore generally beneficial. These questionable arguments tend to justify the immense costs of war, and to rationalize the irresponsible acts of militant leaders on the basis of social need. One comes away with the feeling that war is a pretty good way to get things done, and that it is here to stay.

Leeds allows a little hope by saying this will only happen if "functional substitutes" are not found. Yet I remain unconvinced that the functions Dr. Leeds has named have their implied causal force. Some societies have remained "ossified" in his terms for centuries. Yet others have consistently waged war. Furthermore, we are still a long way from having any objective criterion for the degree of "ossification" at which war would tend to occur, much less be "socially beneficial". Most people are for updating culture lags, but a large and questionable value judgment seems to be involved in formulations which imply that the slaughter of people is a natural price for so-called progress. However, let us not dwell further on these dubious theories.

War in Stateless Societies

The distinguishing criterion of war is the deliberate, approved, legalized killing of people outside of socially defined boundaries. No matter what the scale or social complexity of the units in conflict — no matter how advanced the technology of weaponry and no matter what the intentions, motives, and purposes of combat — all wars share certain basic characteristics of psycho-social process. It is these basic features that I want to explore.

Even if one confines one's attention to wars of stateless (or so-called "primitive" societies), however, considerable differences in the scale of wars are evident. One cannot accurately speak of one unitary phenomenon called "primitive war". For example, in societies at the hunting and gathering level of technology, where social organizations are patrilineal, bands continuously foraging for food (such as Eskimos, South African Bushmen, Pygmies, and Australian aborigines), the frequency and intensity of warfare is very limited. Groups are small due to lack of food supplies and high death rates. Material objectives are few, land is not prized for its fertility, and the life emphasis is upon perpetuating and existing, rather than upon expanding and developing.

As an example of the opposite and upper end of the scale of so-called primitive war we can cite the case of Shaka, the Zulu king who in the incredibly short period of less than 10 years, imposed his rule over a large segment of S.E. Africa. By inventing new enveloping tactics, a new weapon, (the short broad stabbing spear instead of the thrown javelin), and introducing discipline into his army, Shaka expanded from one tribe occupying a territory of 300 square miles to an empire embracing 300 tribes and dominating an area of 80,000 square miles. Battles escalated from dueling fights between individuals, to sustained campaigns, with encounters involving up to 60,000 men and 15,000 casualties (Otterbein, 1967, pp. 351–357). This is a rather unusual case in the world of stateless societies, but by no means unique.

At the opposite extreme is the fighting I referred to earlier, *i.e.* between groups at the simple band level of society. A good example of such warfare is the *atinga,* or avenging party of the Arunta, a group living by hunting and gathering in the harsh desert of Central Australia. The particular *atinga* I will describe was organized by the old men of a band who had determined through mystical procedures that the several recent and unaccountable deaths which had occurred in their group were caused by malevolent magic of a neighboring band. After going through a number of purification rituals, the men painted their bodies, and taking their fighting boomerangs and spears, set out to stealthily approach the enemy group. The other band discovered them, and seeing they were outnumbered, immediately sent out some of their women as evidence of a desire for peace. If the attacking group copulated with the women, it would signify that they would not attack. In this particular case, the offering was rejected, so two men were sent out to confer with the attackers, and two whole days of palavering and negotiations took place. Finally an agreement was reached between the old men of both parties that the battle would be carried out. However, a secret agreement had been made that no one was to be killed by the avengers except three of the young men. It seems that these three men had been causing trouble by not obeying their elders, violating rules for the sharing of meat, taking sexual privileges which did not belong to them, and in general being arrogant. Near dawn the next day a special fire was lit by the old men of the victim group. It was answered by the attackers, who then moved in quickly, speared two of the marked men and retreated, taking their wives as booty. The third victim had smelled trouble and pulled stakes during the night. The elders of the attacked group put up a faked resistance but the only casualties were the two marked men (Spencer and Gillen, 1927).

This example illustrates how war is used as a method of social control in a system of customary law where authority is weak, and legal means of enforcing conformity absent. We can see how the position of the old men was maintained within the band, how the limited conflicts maintained a balance between bands, and how band unity was strengthened.

Despite its alien character in many ways, we do not find this behavior completely incomprehensible. The relationship between motivations of the fighters and the "causes" of the war are more direct than in our modern wars, but they and the social processes involved have a familiar ring to us. For example, the alleged initiating reason for attack was retaliation. Aggression was rationalized in terms of reciprocity, though in our view, the victim band had nothing to do with the losses and frustrations which had upset the attackers. Though the attack was seen in terms of the premise of mystical causation and the consequently logical connection between human hostility and natural calamity, in its own terms it seems just as rational as some of the reasons for the allegedly defensive and preventative wars of our time.

We also understand the bargaining process here. Both groups emerged with some advantage from the violent transaction, though one side had to make the best of a poor bargain and wait for another day for a better payoff. We understand, if we do not approve, of the old men's making the best of their situation by the sly turning of the battle into an execution in the interests of group harmony, while at the same time permitting the dissipation of the aroused hostility of their enemies. They too agreed and understood that it had to be relieved. Analogies could again be found between this behavior and modern international relations — it is a typical dilemma of choice between two evils, with some lives being sacrificed by status-maintaining leaders for the so-called "good" of the group.

Despite such analogies, I want to stress a major source of difference between war of this kind and our own. This is due to the supernatural world view of these societies, a world view in which a sacred realm is an ever present part of every man's existence and which colors all perception. Also, at such a level of technology with great closeness to hills, rocks, and streams, animals and plants of the natural environment, and at the same time with such immediate and constant proximity to the harshly real problems of subsistence living, *death itself* has a different meaning.

The motivations of war are difficult to understand unless one constantly keeps in mind the different meaning which death has in different cultural and historical contexts. Invariably in these stateless societies, because of disease, malnutrition and war, there are high death rates and low life expectancies. Causes of death are generally attributed to supernatural means: usually to witchcraft, sorcery, or enemy spirits. Death is frequent and close, and death by killing is just another way the terrestial phase of spirit is terminated. The fear of death is diminished not only by constant conditioning experience, but by the unshakable assumption that life is eternal spirit, and that man's soul moves back again into the spirit world from which it issued.

The presence of such a world view does not mean that there is no fear of death nor that there is no guilt for killing others. It means only that both fear of death and guilt for killing are diminished in comparison with our own rapidly secularizing society, and seen in a different light.

In primitive societies in contrast to our own, overt motives for fighting are generally directly related to the causes of war — revenge, women, prestige, *etc.* Rarely are they economic, and never are they ideological. Australian aborigines, for example, would ordinarily not conceive of taking the land of others. Each band's land is sacred and spirit infested (Service, 1966). Therefore it is dangerous to outsiders. All groups share the same basic ideological premises regarding the nature of the universe and the moral order. People in these societies often use the existing retaliatory pattern as a vehicle for venting anger arising from death of a close friend or relative. From the point of view of group survival, perhaps even more important than such aggression displacement, these battles, with all the bluffing and demonstrations of ferocity that go with them, assert group

44

autonomy and identity vis-à-vis other groups. Notice is given that it will repel acts against it. In such a situation each act and counter-act serves to remind the members of each group of their relationships to each other, to buttress their unity, and to fence-mend the group boundary.

One of the most common motivations found in the war patterns of primitive societies is the association of ego-validation of manhood with valor and ferocity in combat. Along with this goes the assignment of at least some prestige and power to the successful warrior. There are great variations among stateless societies in the degree to which they have a warrior ethos, but it seems to be very common and is functional for societies which regularly engage in war to develop such a value system. Elevation of bravery and courage to the highest places in the hierarchy of values seems almost an automatic function of war itself, even in societies where peace in valued most highly. Among the peaceful Hopi of Arizona, for example, courage was honored and a warrior society symbolized it in an annual ceremony. The mesa-top villages of these Indians were constantly in danger of Navaho and Apache raiders and survival depended upon being able to strike back. The Hopi warfare orientation was primarily defensive — yet the warrior society provided organized war parties if the group was threatened or attacked. They too collected scalps and slaughtered any women or children encountered in enemy territory.

One of the best firsthand recent accounts of a tribal society emphasizing warrior values has been made by an intrepid young anthropologist, Napoleon Chagnon (1967). This group, who garden root crops in a forest environment of South Venezuela, call themselves *Yanamomo*, and they believe themselves the first and finest people on earth.

The Yanamomo live in villages of 40 to 250 people in an area of low population density — and due to the continuous danger of attack, they try to isolate their villages as far as possible from one another. When villages move, as they frequently do, it is because they have been driven out of the area by a hostile group. In such a case, because of the loss of able warriors, they must often seek refuge with a larger stronger village. They try to avoid this extremity because the host village invariably demands some of their best women in payment for protection. Acquisition of females, made scarce by infanticide, is also the main given reason for initiating hostilities but this motive is just as often used as a pretext for demonstrating personal ferocity and leadership.

Fighting seems to be the main purpose in the life of Yanamomo men, and demonstrations of ferocity their main activity. Men strut around throwing tantrums, bluffing others and venting spite on women or weaker persons. The anthropologist saw women beaten, burned with fire brands and even shot in the buttocks with arrows in outbursts of petulent punishment. He saw reluctant groups of young boys forced to fight by their fathers and then urged on to greater injurious violence as their aggression was aroused by the excitement of contest. Men spend hours memorizing death speeches of defiance which they will utter if mortally wounded in combat, and they even practice defiant noises which they will utter if struck by enemy arrows. The shamans of the village gather daily to take drugs and send their souls into battle against hostile denizens of the other world.

In Yanamomo society there is a great deal of arrogant posturing and utterance of threats. This lets people know that one's threshold of taking offense is low and that any hostile move will provoke immediate violence. There are also frequent ritualized fights without weapons — chest pounding duels in which men stand up and take turns smashing one another until someone falls, often three hours later. Individual duels with clubs are used to settle disputes over such offenses as adultery. In these they take turns beating each other in the head with long heavy sticks. If these duels get out of hand, as they are likely to do, the village chief may use the threat of bow and arrow to stop the two groups of supporters from killing each other.

The real tests of courage among the Yanamomo come in raids on other villages which boys cannot join until they are 18 years old. The mode of attack is to surprise the enemy village at dawn — preferably they may catch someone alone outside the village, perhaps defecating or getting a drink of water. If they make a kill they quickly retreat. If no one is around, they may shoot a volley of arrows into the village and then retreat. As is typical of this level of warfare, casualties in any given raid are not high, but one village Chagnon was studying was raided 25 times during 15 months, and 10 people, or 5% of the population of the village was lost (Chagnon, 1967, p. 141).

I think this somewhat extreme example indicates most clearly the anxiety, fear, and guilt that is really the basis of warrior value systems, no matter how arrogant and defiant the behavior appears. I shall return to this later, but another outstanding feature of primitive war connected with it is the degree to which attempts are made to contain the runaway tendency of fighting, by devising rules. Death and killing are not taken lightly, in spite of supernatural beliefs and warrior values. The anthropologist points out, for example, that the Yanamomo rarely kill women and children in their raids.

It is the proliferation or rules, along with its competitive character, which has prompted so many people to make the obvious analogy of tribal warfare with a game. The warfare complex of the Plains Indians, for instance, has often been referred to as *only* a game. This is an ethnocentric judgment apparently based on the widely held modern assumption that unless conflict is economically motivated, it does not qualify as "true" war. In many of the Plains tribes, the value of personal courage had been carried to such a high point that all other motives were secondary to it. One logical extension of the bravery concept is that the deed of highest merit and prestige is the one in which the greatest risk to life is taken. Therefore, they developed a point system of ranking deeds of bravery. It was more important to score points while risking death than to kill an enemy. Among the Cheyenne, the highest war honor was awarded for counting *coup*, and weapons carried into battle were inversely ranked according to their lethal potential. If a warrior simply touched an armed enemy with a *coup* stick, he had achieved the highest honor. After the *coup* stick, the war club, lance, bow and arrow, and gun ranked in *descending* order. Horses were highly prized, but to steal one from an enemy camp, especially if it was tied to the owner's

46

wrist while he slept, was a much more highly prized action than to capture 100 on the open plains.

In war it is very important to have a clear decision or outcome. Therefore one form of the rules of battle is the method of scoring, of determining the precise outcome of individual feats and group efforts. How does one prove his deeds, many of which take place in the confusion of combat? Counting *coup* was particularly difficult to verify. There had to be witnesses to the touching and agreement among them. Cheyenne warriors would shout "Oh! Haih! " meaning "I am the first", but much time and energy was spent disputing over honors. There was much swearing of solemm oaths and much bragging of one's feats around the fires — within earshot of women and children, of course (Grinnell, 1910).

Most societies have not refined the concept of bravery to such a high point as the Cheyenne, and have used the *killing* as the decisive honor-bestowing deed. The unambiguous decisiveness of death is apparently one reason for this. We, of course, also use the body count as the index of group success; but not having TV and computer coverage — most stateless societies hit upon the notion of bringing back proof of the warrior's bravery. One of the most popular kinds of concrete evidence is the head or scalp of the victim. These trophies, as they accumulate, serve as effective reminders of the owner's bravery and *mana*, or magical power.

Heads are almost always believed to possess sacred power connected with the ghost of the owner, and often this power is believed transferred to the killer, effectively enhancing his status. Also, what could be more humiliating to the still existing enemy spirit than to have his head not only detached from his proper body, but maltreated by his killer? The ancient Scythians, as reported by the Greek traveler Herodotus, used the crania of their most detested enemies as drinking cups with this intention in mind. The *mana* and social ranking of some Melanesian chiefs were calculated by the number of skulls decorating their doors, often ranging from 30 to 1000. In other societies the heads of enemies were set up and ritually asked for forgiveness, or asked favors. The ancient Israelites took heads on special occasions — as when David slew Goliath — but they created a rather unique innovation in trophy-taking by circumcising the fallen infidel and bringing back his foreskin (Weber, 1952, p. 92).

The rules regulating warfare in tribal societies are immensely varied, yet they are always present. There are specific rules of time and place for fighting, and there are almost always some among the enemy who are exempted from killing. There are few groups like the Mongolian tribes of the Middle Ages, or the ancient Israelites, who slew men, women, and children among the enemy. Only the awesome power of modern war has again achieved that degree of indiscriminateness and totality.

Even among such highly warlike tribes as the Yanamomo, and among the fierce warriors of the New Guinea highlands — women and children are frequently exempt. A person who stands in any kind of relationship to a man is usually taboo and carefully avoided in battle. It is a good precaution, therefore, to have the family marriages spread in a number of different groups (Berndt, 1964).

Sometimes there are rules regarding just whom you can use certain weapons upon. The Nuer of the South Sudan have a rule prohibiting the use of spears on anyone in a certain prescribed proximity. Outside the boundary all is fair (Evans-Pritchard, 1940). The duration of battles is also frequently limited by agreed-upon rules. Among the Dane people of New Guinea, nightfall automatically signals a truce, though a battle is not considered concluded until there has been at least one kill on one side or the other (Mathieson, 1962, p. 11).

The relationship between war honor and the rewards of social status in these societies is often clearcut, helping to perpetuate systems of socialization which create powerful motives of self-sacrifice and bravado. Some Melanesian chief's power must be legitimated by continuous military prowess, sacredly validated by accumulation of trophy heads. The Dane "Big Man" warrior is rewarded by sexual access to many women, by better food, and by a much larger sphere of privilege and freedom than the *kepu* — the nonaggressive man who has not killed an enemy (Mathieson, 1962, pp. 15, 16). In some New Guinea tribes, taking a head was prerequisite to marriage, creating a situation where women put a great deal of pressure on sons and lovers to get on with their murdering. Social prestige has repeatedly fed on death in human history.

Ritual in War

In discussing the motives, values, and rules of primitive war, I have often been forced to refer to the supernatural component. I would now like to discuss this ritualistic aspect of war more specifically. A ritual is a system of stereotyped, symbolic activities, and a cultural ritual as opposed to an individual one refers back to some set of traditional ideological premises and ideas, usually to myths concerning supernatural forces. Ritual has the effect of coordinating preparations for action among several organisms. It also functions as a means of organizing the perception of reality, *i.e.* chaos is replaced by order. The repeated sequence of orderly symbolic behaviors reduces the fear and anxiety which is produced in the organism by the often threatening sensory impact of the "buzzing blooming confusion of reality". Thus, ritual has proved adaptive to men and to some animals, and is universally found in human societies (Wallace, 1966, pp. 233–236). It is easily seen why ritual is an inevitable accompaniment of war and an integral part of it. Perhaps in few other situations is reality more inherently chaotic than in the man-made catastrophes called wars.

Preparatory Rituals

Almost all groups perform a series of rituals before they join the enemy in battle which sometimes go on for days or even weeks in advance. We may call these preparatory rituals. The most obvious of these have the overt purpose of protecting the warrior from harm and death. Somehow he must be reassured that he has a reasonable chance of avoiding the fate' of "all those others". Prayers and offerings are among the most common ritualistic attempts to instill such confidence. Giving and wearing of magic amulets, such as Saint Christopher medals, is another.

Many societies have much more elaborate methods. The Jivaro Indians of East Ecuador provide a good example of the complex motivations of ritual belief and values in such societies. They believe that to achieve manhood one must take the head of an enemy and make it into a shrunken talisman. Further achievement of adult status in the society is also bound in great part to killing and head taking. But in order to kill, one must possess an *arutam* soul. This can only be obtained in a vision which is usually experienced near certain sacred waterfalls and through the method of fasting and drinking tobacco water. When the young Jivaro man has seen the apparition — usually an animal, or a disembodied head — he returns to the village to obtain validation of the vision by a dream. When finally convinced that he' has received the *arutam*, he feels a surge of power in his body and senses a new self-confidence. He then believes that he is a superhuman. He is seized with an overwhelming desire to kill and joins a killing expedition. When his war party has surrounded a victim's house, each member of the group ceremonially releases his *arutam* soul into the forest before proceeding with the killing. If they fail they must immediately find another victim, or they will die. Each time they kill they must capture a new *arutam*, but a kind of residue is left from each of them so that the individual's power tends to accumulate. Arutams give protection from violence, poison, witchcraft, or war, so that a man who has killed repeatedly is considered invulnerable and has considerable political and'economic influence (Harner, 1962; Karsten, 1967).

A rather more familiar kind of preparatory ritual for war is *divination*, or forecasting the outcome of the fighting. For example, the Mohave Indians of the Lower Colorado watched for falling stars before a battle. If they fell towards the direction of the enemy, success was assured; if in the opposite direction the expedition was delayed (Fathauer, 1954, p. 98). Divination of this type is of course still common in astrology and was used in recent times by Hitler.

Another type of ritual preparation, warrior ascetism, has just been mentioned — the Jivaro fasting for his *arutam* soul. Ritualized sexual abstinence before a battle is another example so widespread as to be almost universal in primitive and ancient societies. It is usually connected in the people's minds with beliefs concerning the contaminating potency of women and of sexual fluids, but there seems good reason to assume that it also ritually prepares the warrior for the onset of guilt for killing.

Warrior ecstasy is an opposite type of ritually induced preparatory behavior. Historically famous warrior ecstatics are the Berserkers of the Vikings, and the Biblical Sampson who, filled with blood lust, in frenzied, trance-like states performed what seemed to be superhuman feats of mass killing. In some societies such an apparently inspired person often became a leader. More common and less spectacular examples of warrior ecstasy are the war dances in Africa, Asia, Polynesia, and many Indian groups of North America. The war dance, sometimes intensified by drug taking, serves the overt purpose of final emotional preparation to face the spiritual and physical dangers of the enemy. Often these emotion-arousing rituals have the effect of irrevocably committing the individual to bravery and self-sacrifice, for who could show his face if he exhibited cowardice in battle after such extravagantly fierce claims, the vows to kill, and the taunting of the less aggressive? Also, what right would he have to share the spoils in the event of victory?

The great ritual effort to induce commitment may be seen as culturally developed means for overcoming the subconscious repugnance to killing as well as for reduction of fear. The warrior value system apparently needs a great deal of social buttressing, from early training in fierceness through divine validation and many shaming devices to arousal and fear reducing rituals. The great lengths to which societies have to go to stimulate hostile impulses certainly argues against the concept of innate aggression as the cause of war at this social level. Of course, once they have propelled themselves into combat, the interstimulation and provocation of hostile responses come naturally.

Sacrifice is another particularly common form of preparatory ritual, though it also is used after battle. The idea of sacrifice is based on the concept of reciprocity, a most important principle of all tribal social organization. If one regularly maintains one's obligations with the supernatural world through sacrifice, they are expected to return their support in battle. Since spirits frequently like blood, and humans have the most dangerous and sacred blood, human sacrifice has not been uncommon.

The *vow* is a ritual closely related to sacrifice. In war, this is the ritual promise that one will accomplish goals and will not let the self-image down. The vow of revenge, the vow not to return without killing or victory, the vow not to retreat, are common examples. The Plains Indians in battle stuck their spears in the ground as a public symbolic means of vowing to die defending an arbitrary bit of ground rather than retreat. The vow is an evidence of high anxiety and an obvious ritualistic buttress against panic.

Decorations of the body by painting, use of feathers, wearing a uniform *etc.*, are ritualistic preparations both in application, often highly symbolic, and in wearing. This symbolism is not only magically efficacious in warding off the attacks of the enemy, but it serves to set the warrior off from daily life roles. In addition to identifying which team he is on, it puts him into the intermediate sacred and impure status of battle, a liminal zone between spirits and men, in which he will have some disguise and protection against the ghosts of the dead, and against the powers of malevolent sorcery which inhabit the battlefield.

A final example of preparatory ritual is the ritual rehearsal, where the battle is enacted and won symbolically before the war party sets out. The Yanamomo, for example, dramatically sneak up on a dummy set up by the fire, spear it and then jokingly carry out a simulated capture using one of their own women for the victim (Chagnon, 1967). Such rehearsals obviously function as a kind of training maneuver for the young men, though their ostensible purpose is to magically assure success. The Australian aborigines, the Mohave Indians, and many other societies had almost identical kinds of rehearsal rituals (Warner, 1937; Fathauer, 1954).

Battle Ritual

After all has been prepared and battle is actually joined, ritual is still in evidence. Sometimes in societies of tribal level the fighting itself has a highly ritualistic character. The battles of many societies were simply two large groups of men fighting individual duels according to well recognized rules. The idea of champions fighting a battle as symbolic representatives of their groups has also been widespread. It was used in Medieval European times, in ancient Japan, and by the California Indians, among others (Turney-High, 1949). In ancient Israel the combat of champions was apparently used as a form of divination. When David slew Goliath, his personal triumph did not decide the issue but instead gave the armies of Israel the sign that God had blessed them with victory. They fell with new vigor on the hapless Philistines, who apparently had a defeat psychology as a result of the death of their champion (I Samuel, Chapter 17).

During battle, men often obsessively continue to repeat many of the same kinds of individualistic ritual formulae that they have performed before battle. However, in the heat of combat ritual is usually in temporary abeyance.

An exception is the ancient Hebrew's custom of carrying the Ark of the Covenent onto the battlefield as a portable field shrine. God was invoked to arise and lead the forces in battle, returning to the throne after striking down the enemy. The Crusaders and other Christian armies used the cross with similar mystic intent and socially unifying effect. Flags are never so imbued with holiness as when flying above the battling army.

Post-Battle Ritual

But it is after the battle that ritual again reaches a crescendo in primitive societies. We frequently find orgiastic victory dances, in which gloating, bragging and frenzied joyful abandon predominate. Captives are tortured, killed and sometimes eaten. Sexual energies, previously damned up by ascetic taboos, are released, and food and alcohol are consumed in great quantities. This pattern was as typical of the ancient Israelites as it was of the Iroquois or the Zulu. In fact it is recorded in the Bible that the Hebrews' war dance which featured gorging on raw meat and drinking blood (so contrary to normal practice) was shocking to the Philistines.

Much of this behavior is of course a kind of ritualized release of tension and fear. "Victory has ever been strong medicine", as Turney-High, author of a book on *Primitive War* puts it. He further points out that the victory dance restores the upset social equilibrium caused by the war, while at the same time acting as a "rite of passage", *i.e.* a return to the normality of daily life roles which were disturbed by the war (1949, p. 143).

A great part of the ritual following battle is defensive against spirits. Victory is heady, but conversely there are one's own dead to mourn, and retaliatory anger is unleashed on captives as symbolic equivalents of the killers of relatives and friends. Much of such ritual activity seems clearly to indicate the expiation of guilt, even more than it does relief in the freedom from danger, or the ego-inflating claims of triumph. This is expressed in many ways.

The warriors of Murngin of North Australia have an elaborate ritual with the spear which was used to kill. The young warrior who feels anxious and sick with fear is instructed by the old men how to place the point of the spear between his toes, pressing the end of the shaft with his shoulder until the soul of the dead man enters the spear from the ground and proceeds up his leg into his stomach. The warrior then rubs his stomach calling out the name of the man he has killed. He feels much better after this, because the spirit of the deceased has entered his heart and he has now received the life-blood of his enemy. The killer feels much stronger and the old men remark that he has actually grown larger in size. The soul of the dead man later appears to him in a dream, just as the elders said it would, and directs him to follow a certain route in a special kangaroo hunt. The old men examine the kill which he makes, and sure enough, they frequently verify that contrary to superficial appearance the animal is a supernatural one. The warrior then feels relieved enough to resume his normal pursuits (Warner, 1937, pp. 163—173).

Among the pacific Hopi Indians, one who had killed a man carried a burden or ritual responsibility until his own death. All those who had taken scalps had to remain in isolation in the sacred Kiva for 20 days. On the 20th day, a great dance was held around a pole on which all the captured scalps were displayed. The scalps were then symbolically thrown into a sacred crevice in the mountain. This was not the end of the matter though, because each warrior who had taken a scalp thereafter had to attend a nightly ceremony in which one member of their society was delegated to throw sacred cornmeal into the fissure (Ellis, 1951).

Various kinds of ritual penance after killing were widespread in ancient and primitive societies. Fasting, sexual abstinence, and separation were common, as were ritual responsibilities such as sacrifices for vows given. Often the returning warrior was considered sacredly polluted and had to undergo additional purification rituals. Such practices were so widely distributed that to account for them by a theory of diffusion would be impossible for all but the credulous. They are practiced among New Guinea tribesmen, the Southeastern and Southwestern Indian tribes of North America (Natchez, Pima) and many other groups. Some tribes like the Choctaw, Osage and Dakota Indians even had mourning ceremonies for their dead enemies.

To summarize, in stateless or tribal societies, war was endemic. Everyone lived with the immediacy of potentially imminent death. As Marshall Sahlins has recently pointed out, the great organizational problems of such societies (though they did not view it as such) was the problem of *order* (1968, pp. 1—13). A kind of "ordered anarchy" prevailed in the relations between groups both within and between societies. Life was insecure. Peace was rare and precarious. People lived with high toleration of insecurity, and in the absence of superordinate authority, most of their institutions, such as trade and marriage, were oriented towards preserving peace by alliance. War perpetuated itself on the basis of strong group identity and retaliation, supported and reaffirmed by ritual. The reciprocity principle prevailed in death, just as in life. Motives were personal and concrete, rather than abstract ideals — revenge, women, prestige, the aggressive frustration of grief, or defense of life. Fighting for an ideal such as freedom, or a form of government, is alien to tribal people. There is no clash of ideologies making agreement impossible. All parties in an area tend to share the same assumptions

52

about the nature of men, society, and the universe. They also accept the notion of war, its inevitablity, imminence, and regularity as a part of life.

Ritual performs yeoman service under these conditons. It reduces anxiety and fear and instituted confidence, while at the same time giving assurance of ultimate meaning. It reinforces the solidarity of the group by dramatizing its status structure. It strengthens group boundaries, justifies its hostile or defensive activities, and expiates its guilts. It especially supports the warrior values and the warfare process by ceremonially transforming the guilt of killing into self-righteous virtue and strength.

Ritual and Psychopathological Process in War

Despite many obvious differences stemming from the scale, technology, *etc.*, it is tempting to make the analogy between the "ordered anarchy" among the groups of a tribal society and the situation of international politics today. Many parallels seem evident. The same basic processes of group pride (honor), the felt necessity of maintaining a ferocious front, retaliation and counter retaliation, escalation, alliance making and breaking, attempts at rules for battle control, was used as a means for preserving intra-group cohesion, *etc.*, are all operating. Instead of yielding to the temptations to pursue such similarities here, I want to discuss some important common attributes of the warfare process — whether occurring in primitive tribes or modern states.

Such practices as I have been describing are largely ignored by modern theorists of war. They apparently seem too alien and are generally placed in the category of bizarre fighting behaviors of "savages" that do not qualify as "true" war, or "civilized" war (to use what is really a contradiction in terms). But is the behavior of men in modern war so different? How different is a commando raid or a "search and destroy" mission in Vietnam from a raiding party of the Yanamomo, the Dane, the Nuer or the Jivaro? Maybe you too have noticed how the essentially age-old "primitive" tactics of war have suddenly been made respectable and modern, when reinvented by such military "geniuses" as Mao Tse Tung and Che Guevara. Do we see any similarity among Wes Hardin, with 21 notches carved in his six-shooter, the air ace with 29 "kills" marked on his plane, and the New Guinea warrior with his rack of skulls proudly displayed in front of his house?

Let us ask the question how it is that well-bred American middle-class boys, who might at another time be dating, drinking milk shakes, or smoking pot, suddenly find themselves burning children in a Vietnam village (as we witnessed as recently as October 3rd, 1968, on television). What is it that drives a group of boys just out of high school to ruthlessly sever the ears from their fallen enemy to carry as grim talismans (CBS Report, Spring 1968)? How can we account for the boyish gun crew of a naval destroyer carefully lining up the highly magnifying sight of their five inch gun and gleefully blasting out of existence a Korean woman and her cow as they walked along a lonely beach road in 1953? (This was observed by my brother James B. Kennedy.) Is it the sheer brutality of these particular people? Are they conscienceless psychopaths? I think not. Rather, I believe, there is evidence that warfare involves men

53

in a universally *pathological* psycho-social process.

To set the scene for discussing this, let me return to my original definition. *The central core of all warfare is the socially approved or legitimitized killing of persons outside of a defined group.* All groups absolutely prohibit killing within some group boundary larger than the immediate family. They have strongly socialized rules against this, generally with heavy punishment for violation of the rules. Murder is a universal concept which is so much a part of Man's superego that the very thought of commission usually evokes revulsion and dread in the normal society member. Rules regarding murder are universal because social existence is not possible without them.

At the same time, all societies at some level draw a social boundary the other side of which, killing of other human beings is permitted. It is not only permitted, but in many cases enjoined, or at particular times required for attainment of group approval and thereby self-approval. What this means is that *two conflicting moral rules* apply to the *same identical act* — the violent act of taking another's life. The first rule against in-group killing, is learned earliest in connection with acquisition of self-control. The second is learned later in life when the rules against aggression are strongly rooted. The basic and constant psychological feature running through all war is thus the fact that it involves men in what they unconsciously, and sometimes consciously, feel is murder. In addition, it commits them to a situation stimulating many other acts which they have been socialized against. Freud long ago pointed out how among many primitive tribes, such curious customs of mourning for dead enemies and making sacrifices to their spirits suggest the expiation of guilt for having killed them. He said: "We see in them manifestations of repentance, or regard of the enemy, and of bad conscience for having killed him. It seems that the commandment, thou shalt not slay, which could not be violated without punishment, existed also among savages long before any legislation was received from the hands of a God" (1918, p. 53).

It is the basic and universal conflict inherent in this moral dilemma that gives rise to much of the ideology and ritual which are typical of war. In addition to the moral problem involved, and largely because of it, the process of war, once set in motion, is inevitably both psychopathological and pathogenic in nature. I am here advancing a notion of *situational* or *structural* pathology. When people are caught in some particular cultural situations or social structures, they tend to be forced by the dynamics involved to behave in ways technically labeled psychopathological.

How can we say that the situation of war is psychopathological? Let us summarize a few conditions allowing me to make this somewhat controversial statement. Whatever may have been his lofty ideological rationale for entering into a military situation, once committed to combat a man enters a morally inverted world. He is caught in a situation which is most elemental, and in which socially inhibited emotions of fear, hate, revenge, aggression, and love are either required or permitted. Against the enemy they are not only unchecked by normal societal rules, but a basic tacit rule of war is that prohibited behavior is the expected standard. What was punished is now rewarded and approved. In

54

addition, the soldier's ego is on the line, both before the group and before his own ideal self-image. The ego's validation involves the ability to act contrary to a major segment of moral socialization; to selectively act-out carefully repressed antisocial behavior.

This is not to say that such behavior does not carry certain rewards. Being formally released from restraints and suddenly absolved of responsibility for releasing hostility and other desires certainly has rewarding qualities. But in the long run, this creates a greater burden of guilt in the nonpsychopath. With the decline in warrior values characteristic of our time, the conditions leading to this conflict have become progressively intensified for the modern soldier.

The normative commandments of war are: "Thou shalt selectively humiliate, rape, destroy, pillage, deceive, loot and kill, and the greatest of these is to kill". I say "selectively", because the individual must keep compulsive control within his own group. "To the victor belongs the spoils", "Might makes right", and "there's no tomorrow", are some general attitudes of the warrior-soldier. War is inherently a negation of rules and structure – no matter how much men attempt to impose limits and rules upon it. This is why it is often the midwife of social change.

Under such conditions when embarkation on this course of action is begun and there is no turning back, many emotional upheavals occur. Panic may alternate with overwhelming feelings of sorrow, and these followed by desperate anger and vows of revenge. At the same time that realistic self-preservative thought and childish fight and flight impulses alternately crowd the conscious-ness, the psychic work of grief for dead comrades must be suppressed. Yet as friends continue to die around one, the inevitable grief-reactions of guilt, hate and depression are restimulated again and again. The intensive and perpetual threats and challenges to the self-image often evoke either the over-reaction of foolhardy suicidal daring, or they stimulate the depressing ego-deflating shame of realized cowardice. The looming potentiality of death creates acute anxiety states and escapes into fantasy among even the most "normal". Regressive magical thinking typical of early childhood abounds. As Freud postulated, and it seems true, "normal" men going "over the top" often tend to be flooded with infantile feelings of omnipotence as a defense against the immediate proof of their mortality which is an evident reality all around them.

Paranoid suspicions become commonplace and are demonstrated in all kinds of behaviors. Naval officers are pushed overboard, and sergeants "accidently" are shot in the back for a petty slight. Sexual impulses without tenderness are unleashed exploitively on any available object. Manic orgies of gratifying destructiveness alternate with acute remorse in many who would never be labeled manic-depressive in ordinary life At times an overcompensatory ferocity is released, yet later many men even express genuine surprise if accused of "atrocity" or "war crime".

In such a climate, sociopaths, criminals and all kinds of ordinarily socially controlled impulsive individuals find outlets and approved social roles. However, battle forces the average man to the limits of his behavioral repertoire; structurally it induces a set of basically regressive infantile, stressful and irrational behavior patterns, which are permanently destructive to the psychic equilibrium of a certain percentage of men.

Ritual and Other Cultural Defenses

This universal pathological character of war, founded upon its inherent moral dilemma, requires tremendous defensive measures for the mental stability of those gripped within its process. All societies have therefore developed a great paraphenalia of cultural means for protecting the warrior from the self-damaging implications of his antisocial deeds, while at the same time motivating him to perform them.

The kind of stateless societies which I have been discussing used several main strategies of such defense which have been illustrated: The *warrior ethos*, the *supernatural world view*, with its refusal to accept death as final and particularly *rituals* of many kinds. There is still a great deal of ritualism in modern war but due to secularization and changes of religious concepts, much of it does not effectively function in the way described for primitive societies. Looking at motion pictures of the Nazi rallies certainly reminds us, however, that ritual may still be a powerful method of preparation for battle and death. This extreme example reminds us too of the fact that though belief in the mystical power of the spirit world may diminish, a just as strong, irrational, and mystical faith may be aroused by that modern sacred god, the nation-state. In the Nazi case the ancient relationship between warrior values, ritual, and out-group killing was reasserted in vast and startlingly frightening form: being buttressed with methods of modern communications and social control.

It is evident, however, that we now lack most of the preparatory rituals which have been rediscovered again and again throughout history, and which have proved so effective in orienting warriors to their deaths and to their murderous tasks. Warrior asceticism is out of style and so is warrior ecstasy, except perhaps for an occasional Sergeant York or Audie Murphy. It is true that we still have the sacred oath which commits the soldier magically and irrevocably to his role, but it more often appears as a method of reminding the youth that he is threatened by a huge and powerful social control system if he does not comply. We also have lingering practices in various religious faiths which act in the traditional ways. Protestantism provides little besides prayers, but one thinks of Catholic blessings, purification procedures, confession, amulets, rosaries, *etc.* These remnants of the primitive way, however, touch only a part of the modern army and often lack the conviction and potency of the ritual means I have described for nonliterate peoples.

In some ways, too, the training of modern soldiers has a ritualistic character. Training maneuvers, though they obviously serve to increase efficiency, also have a just as important confidence-instilling character, reminiscent of the magical rehearsal. In modern combat, secular disciplinary ritual has replaced sacred ritual, though it is backed by an implicit mystique of duty to a sacred entity, the State. The platitude has it that "there are no atheists in foxholes",

56

and it is obvious that the lack of early training in a warrior ethos, the lack of previous direct exposure to death, the long periods of maturation in a peaceful, affluent, hedonist environment and a lack of ritualistic cushioning often make the shock of confrontation with the immoral, pathological character of battle a desperate experience for the young soldier. One immediate response is apparently to magically grab onto symbols and ideas which formerly had little meaning. However, in the chaos of modern battle, more reliance is placed upon discipline. The compulsive procedures of drill, digging foxholes, moving sandbags, checking weapons, *etc.*, often seem to function more in the typical anxiety-reducing manner of ritual than in their alleged purposes of efficiency.

There is not space here to go into all aspects of modern military ritual. I am sure we all have visions of parades, or of the President pinning more Medals of Honor on more heroes than we ever had before. Military protocol, victory parades, and memorial day ceremonies are obvious examples of the persistence of ritual in connection with war. Nevertheless, you will probably admit that both pre- and post-battle rituals of our times are now pale and empty in comparison with those of nonliterate peoples. The powerful ritual means for expiating guilt have been largely forgotten by societies, who instead go to extraordinary lengths to hide the implications of their murderous acts from those called upon to perpetrate them. The killing of an enemy by firing squad, however, is a beautiful example of a remaining ritual which attempts to deny any guilt or need of expiation, by dramatically reaffirming the moral righteousness of murder. There is perhaps no more effective way of absolutely rejecting the implications of warfare actions than to publicly re-enact the extirpation of evil with the full legitimation of sacred state power. The physical acting out by dramatic ceremony again serves to publicly and ritually insist upon the absolute justice of previous actions about which there is a great moral doubt. This is perhaps the epitome of "the ritual of intergroup murder".

The modern soldier has had his ritual defense mechanisms greatly diminished in effectiveness due to the historical evolution of modern societies. At the same time his destructive potential has been enormously increased. His knowledge of other peoples and therefore his "sympathy quotient" has also increased, often making *conscious* the ambivalent conflict and guilt which was always latent in the dilemma of war. All traditional sources of sacredness are devaluing before the onslaught of evolving science and new world-awareness. Death itself takes on a new meaning both for the self and for the conception of the enemy. The knowledge that it is final becomes more and more difficult to wish away and to keep out of consciousness. In the face of the growing murder-potential of all armies and the continuance of war, it has been necessary to supplement our empty ritual methods with others. These I call *cultural insulating procedures* since they serve to disguise the true face of war and to impose psychological distance between the murderer and his victims.

One of these, "verbal magic", has always been an important method of insulating the conscience from its acts and their consequences, though modern forms attempt to deny their essentially magical character. A most obvious universal example has been one of my main themes here, the semantic manipulation which attempts to mask the fact that deliberate killing is murder. Another almost universal form is the definition of all aggressive attacks as defensive in nature, that is, as righteous, justified retaliation. Under verbal magic also falls what Lawrence Frank and others have called the "dehumanization of the enemy". A widespread example of this was the simple definition of those one wanted to or had to kill, as "animals". This still survives in such practices as calling the enemy of other races gooks, wogs, *etc.*, making it easier to exterminate them.

A perhaps more modern form of such magic is by verbally devaluing or de-emotionalizing an act. For example, a common phrase of our military forces is to speak of all murderous and destructive activities as "doing a job". "getting the job done", *etc.* This removes the implications of violence and places killing and destruction within the calm and admirable category of productive labor. One does not then mind going into the "service" or getting paid for his "services" at the end of the month. The classification of killing as work is not unlike the magical classification of some murders of civilians or members of one's own group as "accidents".

In a slightly different category of verbal magic are those defensive rationalizations which invoke some set of higher values as justification for killing. Often these refer to a social control system which compelled the behavior on pain of severe punishment. "I did it on the Führer's orders" is a typical form of excuse for abdication of responsibility here. Ordinarily condemned behavior is then transformed into simple duty.

Another type of insulating method may be called "distancing devices". Here I am referring to all those physical and psychological means by which people remove themselves or are removed from the real "business" of combat — the bloody killing of people — yet at the same time remaining participants, supporters or even directors of the deadly process in one way or another. Most obvious here, of course, is the long distance weapon, permitting killing without coming into sensory range of the victim in his living human vitality. We needn't speak of this further. It is obvious how, with our scientific methods, deaths are reduced to emotionless statistics. The fact that it is even *possible* to bomb cities, killing thousands of innocent women and children, is testimony to the tremendous effectiveness of such distancing techniques. Mass homicide is not only made possible by increasing the efficiency of murdering, but by the complete impersonalization of killing and torture, the almost total separation of the actor from the consequences of his violent behavior.

In discussing such distancing, we cannot forget those separations which result from the inherent characteristics of organization but which are exploited by the role occupants. It is commonplace that the higher the rank of the officers, the less the personal risk. This is dubiously rationalized by their allegedly greater value, but we can point to another effect of it. The higher rank, the further one is removed from the sensing of the actual lethal consequences of his action. The old enlisted man's suggestion for stopping wars by placing all high officers from both sides in the front lines has considerable merit from this point of view. The visions we have of bemedaled portly generals playing chess with armies of our sons also has some validity, despite *their* often genuine attempts at concern, or *our* stupendous efforts to believe in them. The separation of decision makers (or Force Wielders as I like to call them) from the rank and file is a function of organizational complexity but is also a major factor in the causation of modern wars. It is only in the rarified atmospheres of general staff headquarters where decisions affecting the deaths of millions may be made with sufficient dispassion and objectivity, where blood and brutality may be kept from intruding on the "rational" decision-making process.

We should not forget the role of our mass media in our list of mechanisms of insulation. As we idly switch our TV from Gunsmoke to pro-football to a "search and destroy" mission in Vietnam, the distinctions between entertainment and the reality of grimly warring men cannot help but become blurred. History books have always performed this insulating function by depicting war as a detached list of places, battles and leaders, in which the end result was emphasized and our good-guy heroes won more than they lost.

Conclusion

In our modern society with its inefficient incalculation of warrior values, its widespread disillusion and its growing awareness of the implications of actions, more and more effort is required to induce men into the pathological process of war. Threat of shame at the local level is still an important way of accomplishing this, but it has lost much of its effectiveness. Killing has progressively lost its meaning in the ego-validation of young men, and the State has gradually lost much of its sacred luster. For sometime now it has been necessary for the Force Wielders of large-scale societies to coerce men into the warfare process. Lately, in addition to force, we have seen more use of promises of positive rewards such as education, income and adventure. Overt seduction is added to coercion.

(handwritten margin note: but in Yugo it is local)

In our chaotic times the rigidly structured life of the military offers other rewards too, such as relief from the responsibilities of decision making and freedom, or action for the restless and bored. For the floundering it holds out the vague hope of finding order and meaning, but once committed to battle, whether one has arrived by seduction, coercion or motives of escape, the individual finds himself trapped within the age-old morally inverted pathological process. The motives and defenses of typical warriors are inevitably brought into play: the aggression, the retaliation, the felt necessities of validating manhood before the self and the group, and the greed for women and plunder. All the infantile, impulsive and obsessive processes of the warfare situation become activated. The Force Wielders well realize that these processes will take place and in fact are necessary to the continuance of armed conflict. They intuitively understand the tremendous need to justify acts after they have been done. They know the importance of getting a man "committed" so that he will not be able to turn back. They try to provide the ceremonial honoring and the ideological myths which will enable the rationalization of murder.

But we must not imply an indictment of the Force Wielders as unmitigated

59

exploiting villains. There are some of those to be sure, but the Force Wielders are also Responsibility Holders, and they too are caught mostly unwittingly in the powerful current of psycho-social process. As Kenneth Boulding has eloquently reminded us, the modern state is losing much of its foundation of sacred legitimacy — and war with its call for unanimity and acceptance of the State's value is a powerful means of preserving it. Once engaged, however, they are caught in the "sacrifice trap", as he calls it. "Once we have made sacrifices for anything . . . it becomes very hard to admit we have made the sacrifices in vain, for this would be a threat to our identity. Consequently the making of sacrifices builds up an integrated relationship which justifies them. It is not only the blood of martyrs that is the seed of the church; the blood of soldiers is the seed of the sacred state." He goes on to propose that the only "rational" purpose of the present war in Vietnam is the killing of young Americans to refurbish the sacredness of the national state (1968, pp. 24, 25).

I would not view such a purpose as rational, nor do I think it is an explicit policy. Nevertheless, Boulding has pointed to a significant process and has put his finger on an important determinant in the perpetuation of war today. One implication to me is that, despite the important roles which nation-states have played in bettering our world, no matter how much we cherish our loyalties to these sacred entities, they must be eliminated from the world scene. The nationalistic ideals which have served so many leaders so well are now rapidly becoming the cancer which will destroy us all. Modern weaponry no longer permits us the luxury of maintaining our primitive system of religious nationalism, feeding on war.

It has often been pointed out that among tribal groups the boundaries between truly significant social groups are those based on the attitudes and rules which define killing within them as murder and killing outside of them as war. The significance of boundaries between nation-states today is based upon precisely the same principle. One major trend of world history has been towards a pushing outward of the murder/war boundary lines. It is the task of men in our time to finally admit the archaic arbitrariness of such lines and awaken to the implications of the ancient hypocrisy that makes border lines into barriers and perpetuates war.

BIBLIOGRAPHY

Ardrey, R., *The Territorial Imperative*, Athenum, New York, 1966.

Berndt, M., Warfare in the New Guinea Highlands, *Am. Anthropologist*, 66, No. 4, Part 2 (1964) 183–203.

Bohannon, P., *Law and Warfare*, The Natural History Press, New York, 1967.

Boulding, K., Divine Legitimation and the Defense Establishment, *Humanist*, January-February (1968) 21–25.

Chagnon, N., Yanamomo Social Organization and Warfare, in M. Fried, M. Harris and R. Murphey(eds.), *War: The Anthropology of Armed Conflict and Aggression*, The Natural History Press, New York, 1967, pp. 109–160.

Ellis, F.H., Patterns of Aggression and the War Cult in Southwestern Pueblos, *Southwestern Journal of Anthropology,* 7(1951) 177—201.

Evans-Pritchard, E.E., *The Nuer,* The Clarendon Press, Oxford, 1940.

Fathauer, G.H., The Structure and Causation of Mohave Warfare, *Southwestern Journal of Anthropology,* 10(1954) 97—118.

Freud, S., *Totem and Taboo,* Random House (Modern Library Paperback), New York, 1918.

Grinnell, G.N., Coup and Scalp Among the Plains Indians, *Am. Anthropologist,* 12(1910) 296—310.

Harner, M., Jivaro Souls, *Am. Anthropologist,* 64, No. 2 (1962) 258—272.

Karsten, R., Blood Revenge Among the Jivaro Indians of Eastern Ecuador, in P. Bohannan (ed.), *Law and Warfare,* The Natural History Press, New York, 1967.

Leeds, A., The Functions of War, in J. Masserman (ed.), *Violence and War: With Clinical Studies,* Vol. VI of *Science and Psychoanalysis,* Grune and Stratton, New York, 1963, pp. 69—82.

Lorenz, K., *On Aggression,* Harcourt, Brace and World, New York, 1966.

Malinowski, B., in L. Bramson and G.W. Goethals (eds.), *War: Studies from Psychology, Sociology and Anthropology,* Basic Books, New York, 1968.

Mathieson, P., *Under the Mountain Wall,* Viking, New York, 1962.

Otterbein, K., The Evolution of Zulu Warfare, in P. Bohannan (ed.), *Law and Warfare,* The Natural History Press, New York, 1967.

Sahlins, M., *Tribesman,* Prentice Hall, Englewood Cliffs, N.J., 1968.

Service, E., *The Hunters,* Prentice Hall, Englewood Cliffs, N.J., 1966.

Spencer, B., and F.J. Gillen, *The Arunta* (2 vols.), Macmillan and Co., London, 1927.

I Samuel, *The Holy Bible* (King James Version), Universal Book and Bible House, Philadelphia, 1944.

Turney-High, H.H., *Primitive War: Its Practice and Concepts,* University of South Carolina Press, Columbia, S.C., 1949.

Wallace, A.F.C., *Religion: An Anthropological View,* Random House, New York, 1966.

Warner, W.L., *A Black Civilization,* Harper and Brothers, New York, 1937.

Weber, M., *Ancient Judaism,* translated by Hans H. Gerth and Don Martindale, Free Press, New York, 1952.

White, L., *The Science of Culture,* Grove Press, New York, 1949.

The Role of Warfare in History

JERE CLEMENS KING

Until the 19th century, war was traditionally included with death, pestilence and famine to comprise the four horsemen of the Apocalypse. These scourges were viewed, more or less fatalistically, as the punishment of an inscrutable but wrathful God, or as the cruel caprice of nature. But by the middle of the 19th century, Science had made sufficient advances in medicine and agriculture to create at least the potentialities of controlling or eliminating plague, lengthening the life span, rationally limiting the size of the population and producing enough food to avoid famine. Only the scourge of war seemed to defy the possibilities of conscious control.

The literature of warfare is enormous, but most of it is epic, saga, or drum-and-trumpet recitative of the sacred origins or heroics of the ingroup, whether that ingroup be clan, creed, nation, race or class. Only within the last 200 years has the study of the causes of war and of their elimination begun to supplant traditional preoccupation with war's course or conduct.

We may draw some comfort from the analogy of economics. For centuries the economic environment was thought to be at the mercy of blind chance or at the whim of mammon, until recent economists such as John Maynard Keynes developed the regulative mechanisms which have made possible the nationally and internationally monitored economies of our day. When it is fully comprehended that, with modern technology being what it now is, the elimination of the causes of war may very well be the precondition of our survival, then, and perhaps only then, will the focus of attention be shifted from preoccupation with war's course and conduct to a sustained and systematic study of its causes and their removal.

War has been broadly defined as: "The use of physical force to settle disputes between organized groups". Professor Quincy Wright, author of the classic *Study of War*, has divided the history of war into five great periods.

The first of these was animal war. Animals are fortunate in being spared mankind's by now limitless means of killing, for apart from stone-throwing monkeys and club-brandishing higher apes, animals use only their bodily equipment to kill. Lethal fighting between animals of the same species is very rare, and nonlethal hostility is generally confined to fights between males for the control of females, or for protection of habitation sites, or for group leadership. Among animals of different species, the predators attack other species for food, and the animals attacked generally try to escape rather than fight back. A willingness to commit mass homicide among his own species is an "honor" left only to man.

Primitive man, presumably higher than the apes but definitely lower than the angels, used what was at his disposal to kill in the hunt and in war. Employing stones, clubs, spears, bows and arrows for attack, and animal skins and shields for defense — organized politically along the lines of blood relationship, clan, village, or tribe — primitive man usually fought to vindicate his ingroup's mores — or so to speak, to defend the old Altamira cave's "way of life" — rather than for economic gain or political conquest which became important war aims only with the evolution of herding and agriculture. When this stage of development was reached, the ingroups of clans or tribes were integrated into kingdoms or federations; warriors became specialized; killing implements were more cunningly contrived; and economic and political motives became more predominant. Man was now ready to cross the threshhold of "civilization".

Professor Wright points out that in the civilization stage, characterized by the invention of the alphabet, systematic agriculture, and the rule of defined territories by political hierarchies, war was taken over by a professional class for purposes of plunder, land acquisition, trade, or the spreading of a religion or an ideology. The horse and chariot were put to military use, armies were drilled into disciplined masses, cities were fortified, and siege engines, such as the ballista, were invented. Civilizations usually began with numerous city states which struggled with one another until the smaller city states were conquered and absorbed by the larger. These latter had the advantages of more efficient public administration, the tactics of the mass charge of trained phalanxes or legions, and the use of siege belfries against walled cities. Alliances and power balancing began to emerge, and great empires arose in Egypt under Thutmose I, in Mesopotamia under Tiglath-Pileser, in the Middle East under Alexander, under Asóka in India, under Ch'in in China and under Julius Caesar in the Mediterranean. These empires were eventually sapped by overcentralization, corruption, and the alienation of their internal proletariats, and they fell before the onslaughts of external barbarians. Wars thus led first to the integration of a civilization and later to its destruction.

Wright lists eight great wars which had decisive effects on our Western civilization.

(1) In the 4th century B.C., Alexander the Great conquered the territory between India and Egypt by use of the Macedonian phalanx and siege egines.

(2) By the Age of the Antonine Caesars, the Romans had conquered 150 million people with their infantry legions and cavalry.

(3) Through superior cavalry tactics, Attila the Hun and subsequently Germanic tribes overran much of the Roman Empire which was weakly defended by barbarian mercenaries.

(4) Beginning in the 7th century, the Arab horsemen of Mohammed achieved whirlwind conquests of lands extending from Iran to France until Charles Martel defeated the Moors at the Battle of Tours in 732.

(5) In the 8th century, Charlemagne's armored knights on horseback and his militia set up an ephemeral empire in what is now France, Germany and

Italy, which survived as the loosely articulated Holy Roman Empire.

(6) From the 9th to the 11th centuries, the sea-roving Vikings invaded England, Normandy, Iceland, Greenland, Italy and even America.

(7) The Crusaders set up a short-lived kingdom in Palestine in their wars against Islam and Byzantium between 1095 and 1270.

(8) England's attempts to conquer France in the Hundred Years' War, in which the British invaders used feudal armies, longbowmen, pikemen, and naval transport, served as a catalyst to activate nationalism in both France and England.

Wright is convinced that as regards the causation of these wars, ideology seemed dominant in the conquests of Islam, of Charlemagne, of the Crusaders and of the British and French in their national conflicts of the Hundred Years' War. The economic motive was strong in the plundering raids of the Huns and the Vikings, and in many of the Muslim warriors and Crusaders. The Huns and the Norsemen dispensed with any pretense of legal or juridical niceties in their depredations.

Gunpowder, when introduced from China, ushered in the Age of Modern War. It gave the offensive an advantage over the static defenses of the castles of the feudal nobility. In the interest of establishing order and limiting private wars, the new national monarchs made common cause with the clergy and the bourgeoisie. By equipping plebeian infantrymen with firearms, the kings and the middle classes were able to prevail over the feudal lords and thereby establish the modern nation-states. War was two-edged. It was often devastating in the regions actually fought over (as in the Germanies during the ferocious Thirty Years' War of religion), but at the same time warfare spurred production in mining, metallurgy and transport in uninvaded territories. It was in the Thirty Years' War that Swedish King Gustavus Adolphus conclusively demonstrated the effectiveness of the musket's firepower against massed pikemen. He improved standards of discipline, and substituted linear tactics for mass formations — innovations which the French soon adopted. The armies of Louis XIV also devised modern staff organizations and permanent tactical units. Louis XIV had his cannon stamped with the peremptory engraving: *ultima ratio regum*, which might be loosely translated as, *the king's last word*. In the 18th century, Frederick the Great improved upon linear tactics by increasing the rate of fire through intensive drilling of his Prussian infantry. He emphasized mobility and maneuver by introducing horse-drawn cannon and by reinforcing his infantry with supporting artillery. The British army of the 18th century emulated Frederick's rigid discipline but not his adroit use of mobility and maneuver, and this neglect contributed to the victory of American colonial minute men and militia over the British regulars and regimented Hessian mercenaries.

One of history's most brilliant displays of military prowess was the career of Napoleon Bonaparte, who was said to have originated only one thing — a knack at winning victories — at least until his defeat at Waterloo. Napoleon utilized the vast conscript armies raised by the First French Republic to put into practice copy book exercises of wide strategic envelopment (or the turning movement) and the defensive-offensive maneuver. And in the wake of his conquests, extending from Spain to Russia, Napoleon's armies exported the French Revolutionary concepts of nationalism, and the supplanting of feudal regimes by relatively liberal, bourgeois, modern administrations.

Far surpassing the carnage of the Napoleonic wars was the Taiping Rebellion in China in which 20 million people lost their lives between 1850 and 1864.

Within Western Civilization, the costliest conflict between 1815 and 1914 was our American Civil War in which 600,000 died. This struggle advanced the military art, in addition to preserving the American Union, ending chattel slavery and submerging for a century what was once thought to be exclusively Southern racism. During the Civil War the railway, the telegraph, the steam engine and the iron-clad ship were all put to military use. These logistical innovations, as well as the newly invented rifled weapons and the "scorched earth" strategy of General Sherman's march through Georgia, introduced the modern epoch of Total War.

Even bloodier than the Taiping Rebellion and the American Civil War was the First World War, in which not only the armed manpower but the regimented economies of entire nations were deployed against one another. There was an almost universal expectation in the opening weeks of the war that the massed infantry offensive, accompanied by mobile artillery, would prove quickly decisive, as in the Austro-Prussian and Franco-Prussian Wars. But after the Battle of the Marne and the Race to the Sea, combat in Western Europe settled into four years of trench warfare characterized by sporadic offensives which proved suicidal and by "nibbling operations" of ceaseless attrition. The new devices of the machine gun, barbed wire networks, recoil mechanisms, the airplane used for reconnaissance and the automobile for logistics all proved to be to the advantage of the defensive. In the war years between 1914 and 1918, 9 million soldiers and 30 million civilians lost their lives.

The most lasting results of the First World War were the emergence of messianic Communism in Russia, and the accelerated rise of America as a major world power. The physical damage of the war was repaired sooner than expected, but unfortunately it turned out not to be the "War to End War". The central flaw of the Treaty of Versailles was that it neither crushed nor conciliated defeated Germany but rather scotched and irritated that formidable military power without depriving it of the means of retaliation.

The Second World War, begun by Germany, cost no less than 17 million military lives and 34 million civilian. Its monetary cost has been estimated at more than 1 trillion dollars. This was the first war in which strategic aviation played a major role. Much of the fighting in the Pacific was done by planes operating from aircraft carriers. The Luftwaffe, the Royal Air Force and the American Air Force, in their terrifying, saturation bombing raids upon the major cities of England, Germany and Japan, carried mass death to civilians hundreds of miles behind the land or sea fighting fronts. The chief consequences of the Second World War were first, the spread of Communism behind the victorious Russian armies in their advances into Eastern Europe and into Northern China and Korea; second, the polarization of the world between the two superpowers, the Soviet Union and the United States; and third, the development of nuclear weapons. Atomic armament, it was thought at first, rendered obsolete all previous theories of warfare or perhaps even war itself. A quantum jump in the techniques of mass violence had been made. The fact that the atomic bomb is more than "just another weapon" is obvious to many, if not to General Curtis Le May. With the spread of these nuclear weapons to Britain, Russia, France and China, and with the development of long range jet bombers, nuclear submarines and intercontinental ballistic missiles, entire nations equipped with weapons of *total* destruction now stand poised at point blank range vis-à-vis one another.

Professional soldiers, left to their own rather simple devices, could never have produced complex weapons of such apocalyptic power. Atomic weapons, as we all know, were the ingenious inventions of such distinguished scientists as Einstein, Bohr, Fermi, Oppenheimer and Teller. The American military historian Theodore Ropp has observed that weapons competition is not new, but only recently has technological change been rapid and continuous enough to make the scientist as important in war as the soldier or the statesman. Even the introduction of gunpowder was so gradual that the development of fire weapons was discontinuous. The 19th century invented the method of invention. For the first time scientists and engineers turned their attention to a disciplined attack on one difficulty after another. The outcome has been the perfecting of a military technology fully capable of destroying civilization, slowly through the long range effects of radioactive fallout, if not instantly from the direct blasts of nuclear explosions. But so far, the nuclear deterrent has at least deterred the actual use of these weapons, although not the use of the more old fashioned weapons.

There have been some curious consequences of this state of world tension. Since the Cold War between Moscow and Washington began soon after the shooting war between the Allies and the Axis ended, continuous military preparedness, for the first time, became an integral part of the "American Way of Life". For example, the draft has lasted from 1940 until today. And between 1946 and 1968, there have been more than 30 hostile incidents in various countries around the globe in which as many as 500 deaths each occurred. Since the Second World War, localized wars have been fought in China, Greece, Korea, Hungary, Tibet, Algeria, Indonesia, the Congo, on the Indian-Pakistani borders, on Israel's borders, in Nigeria, and now in Vietnam, Laos and Cambodia — all as if the atomic bomb had never been invented. War may be theoretically obsolete, but its practitioners are not as yet suffering from any visible signs of technological unemployment.

Among the side effects of the continuing tensions of the Cold War has been the appropriation by Congress of vast sums of money to foster research and development in scientific, engineering and other fields related to "military defense". "Defense" has been so broadly construed as to include "potential" problem areas, such as the newly emergent, underdeveloped countries, which *might* become theaters of actual conflict in the Cold War. A cornucopia of research grants has been lavished upon University departments of physics, chemistry, engineering, mathematics, astronomy, medicine, and even such seemingly nonmilitary fields as African Studies, Latin American Studies, Eastern

66

European Studies, Near Eastern Studies — not to mention the more plausible "enemy" fields such as the Russian, Chinese and South East Asian.

Presumably, and by the same token, if our "War in the Streets" heats up enough, perhaps civil or racial war grants may be "spun off" (as the current academic cant has it) to the monetary advantage of Sociologists, Political Scientists, Urban Historians, Black Historians, Military Historians, Anthropologists, City Planners, Psychologists, Psychiatrists, Criminologists, Law Professors, and perhaps even for the second round, Chemists, who might be called upon to improve the restraining properties of Mace.

To take an example close at hand of a University which, with the best of intentions, has become a monetary beneficiary of the more time-honored international conflicts and tensions, our own University of California now derives more than half of its annual income from the Atomic Energy Commission which has certainly not ignored the questions of weaponry, whether or not it has made their development its exclusive preoccupation. The University of California still directs Los Alamos and Livermore. In short, the academic community has unwittingly acquired a vast vested interest in what can only be described as "military socialism". In the wildly improbable event of "peace suddenly breaking out tomorrow" (which the Russians in Czechoslovakia have precluded quite as much as the Americans in Vietnam), entire academic departments would be at least temporarily disoriented, if not totally unhinged.

General Dwight D. Eisenhower warned, in his farewell address as President on January 17th, 1961, that America must guard against the "acquisition of unwarranted influence ... by the military-industrial complex" because of the "potential for the disastrous rise of misplaced power". He also cautioned against the "prospect of domination of the nation's scholars by federal employment".

Expanding upon this issue, Senator J. William Fulbright emphasized the insidiousness of the military-industrial-academic complex.

"The bonds between goverment and universities are not the result of a conspiracy", he said, but can be explained by the fact that "professors like money and influence as much as businessmen, workers and politicians".

The military-industrial complex is the result rather than the cause of American military involvements around the world.

"But, composed as it is of a vast number of citizens — not tycoons or 'merchants of death' but ordinary, good American citizens — whose livelihood depends on defense production, the military-industrial complex has become an indirect force for the perpetuation of our global military commitments."

The war ties between government and industry are even closer, at least in California, than those between government and the Universities. The historian James L. Clayton, in his study, *The Impact of the Cold War on the Economies of California and Utah, 1946–1965*, states that from 1950 to 1963, 661,000 new jobs were created in California's manufacturing industries and that more than 60% of these were in aerospace industries. If one adds to each direct defense job, whether it be in aircraft, ordnance, electronics or shipbuilding, two additional indirect jobs — a conservative assumption — then over 1.5 million workers or about one third of *all* nonagricultural employees in California in recent years have been dependent on continued defense expenditures. Since the outbreak of the Cold War, more than 50 billion defense dollars have been spent in Los Angeles County alone. Professor Clayton states that defense spending was the main factor in the rapid growth of Los Angeles, Orange, Santa Clara, Santa Barbara, Riverside, San Diego and San Bernadino Counties. Concomitant with the enormous influx of "defense workers" into these parts of California has been the sudden and dramatic increase in the problems of congestion, suburban sprawl added to urban blight, rising crime, clogged highways and smog. Scant wonder that some of our citizens sigh for a bygone age.

Well might we long for the past when we reflect upon America's position in the world today. We are bogged down in Vietnam in what is so far the longest and perhaps the most unpopular war in our history. We are appropriating no less than 72 billion dollars for defense for the next fiscal year. We are plagued with festering ghettos which are internal colonies whose inhabitants sometimes threaten a civil or racial war of liberation. We have alienated our youth with the contradictions of our democratic preachment and racist practice, and with our affluence in the midst of dismal squalor. We are able to blow up the world with our most spectacular weapons, or to eliminate all life in entire cities without damage to property through use of our new ingenious nerve gases or bacteriological weapons, but apparently we cannot end the war in Vietnam or make all of our citizens feel a sense of community. In this state of affairs we were recently urged to concentrate upon the politics of joy. And for executive leadership we have been allowed to choose either this same evangelist of joy, or a weathercock politician who would swing around in any wind to his advantage or a Yahoo demagogue who would make General Curtis Le May the nation's Vice President.

The other superpower, Soviet Russia, meanwhile drops the pretense of ever having evolved beyond its dictatorial and militaristic origins and invades Czechoslovakia to crush a regime which was trying to reconcile a socialized economy with respect for civil liberties. Quite apart from our own increasing dependence upon military socialism and its economic "spin off" to help maintain our inequitable prosperity, this recent Russian atavism would be enough in itself to renew the Cold War full blast. So back to the old Cold War clichés!

It seems to me that America now has, in theory, three choices in its foreign and defense policies. It can continue in its present thankless role of trying to be the world's policeman, attempting, for example, to break up the fight in the back alley of Vietnam; or it could pull back to a Fortress America and try to deter external attack by its world-girdling nuclear rocketry, and thereby free its army to be retrained for use at home in fighting Blacks and hippies to "maintain order in the streets" and protect property; or it could scale down its present nebulous treaty commitments to 42 countries, retaining as allies the more strategically important and viable nations and replacing most military aid with economic aid through an agency like the World Bank. Moreover, it could learn to welcome social evolution and even popular revolutions abroad, if the latter course were the only way to replace reactionary dictatorships. The

68

important thing is to try, within reason, to prevent the rise of hostile, undemocratic and expansionist regimes by encouraging underdeveloped peoples to strive for a middle way between military dictatorships of the Right and the fraudulent "dictatorships of the proletariat" of the Moscow or Peking variety. America should welcome the efforts of a Dubcek as much as we should oppose those of a Patakos or a Papadopoulos.

What of relying upon the good offices of the United Nations? This organization has proved effective when the superpowers of America and Russia were on the same side of a dispute but of little use when they were on the opposite sides, as in the Israeli-Arab conflict. A pale shadow of a world government in an age of continuing nationalisms, the U.N. must nevertheless be kept alive, for a supranationalist entity is the logical next step in governmental evolution.

Such a median course between that of world policeman and neo-isolationist would allow us to divert from our present astronomical defense budget billions of dollars annually for rebuilding our cities, for providing education and jobs for the impoverished minorities and for winning back our alienated youth. As for our armed forces, they should be scaled down to a size commensurate with the more realistic policy commitments which we should adopt. And, in my opinion, the present draft, which rakes into the armed forces chiefly Blacks, Mexican-Americans and poor Whites, and only recently, some graduate students, should be replaced by an equitable and efficient draft lottery. For, unhappily, there is as yet no acceptable world government with an effective world police force.

BIBLIOGRAPHY

Aron, R., *War and Industrial Society*, Oxford University Press, Oxford, 1958.

Fuller, J.F.C., *A Military History of the Western World* (3 vols.), Funk and Wagnalls, New York, 1954–56.

Kotzsh, L., *The concept of War in Contemporary History and International Law*, E. Droz, Geneva, 1956.

Montross, L., *War Through the Ages*, Harper, New York, 3rd ed., 1960.

Preston, R.A., S.F. Wise and H.O. Werner, *Men in Arms: A History of Warfare and Its Interrelationship with Western Society*, F.A. Praeger, New York, 1956.

Ropp, T., *War in the Modern World*, Duke University Press, Durham, N.C., 3rd ed., 1965.

Spaulding, O.L., H. Nickerson and J.W. Wright, *Warfare*, Harcourt, Brace and Co., New York, 1937.

Vagts, A., *A History of Militarism*, W.W. Norton and Co., New York, 1937.

Wright, Q., *Study of War* (2 vols.), University of Chicago Press, Chicago, Ill.,1942.

Psychic Factors in the Causation of Recurrent Mass Homicide

MAURICE N. WALSH

It seems evident from recent history that we need a new approach and a reassessment of our attitude toward the recurrent episodes of mass murder which have, like a disease of society, swept over the world since time immemorial. I feel that the term "war" should be abolished as meaningless, and its seems to me that the term "recurrent mass homicide" might be substituted. Even the old military theorist Klausewitz, certainly no lover of peace, recognized that war is an extension of policy by violent means. This implies that we have a constant atmosphere of conflict which becomes violent only at intervals. Therefore "recurrent mass homicide" seems to me to be more meaningful because the term "war" implies, it seems to me, that we know what we are talking about, and I am not at all sure that we really do.

At any rate, a new approach would certainly have to include some new thinking. When I say this I do not wish to minimize the importance of the economic, historical, sociological, anthropological, political and military studies which are necessary to an understanding of the recurrent outbreaks of mass murder which periodically devastate mankind like a recurrent plague. However, it seems evident to me that in all these studies an important factor has been left out of consideration and that is the emotional factor. This is indeed remarkable to anyone who has participated in the combat zone in a war in which emotions run rampant. By this I refer to the recurrent violent outbreaks of mass emotion throughout history, of which recurrent mass homicide is one consequence. I feel that leaving any one of these factors out of consideration dooms our effort to understand and hopefully to ultimately so adequately comprehend the origins of these recurrent episodes of mass murder that these origins may be finally understood and the holocausts thus prevented.

Certainly this repetitive plague of recurrent mass homicide is a complex phenomenon, like a plague of society which periodically sweeps over the world. Most of the great plagues of mankind have now been conquered and in fact they are merely memories. We do not hear today of recurrences of black plague, of typhoid fever, of yellow fever or of any of the other plagues which formerly causes millions of deaths. They have been conquered by the application of the scientific method, first to the study of their origins and finally to their prophylaxis, and as a result they do not exist any more.

But the scientific method has really not yet been fully applied to a study of the phenomenon of recurrent mass homicide. We might ask, why the emotional factor has been so totally neglected in attempting to understand the phenomenon? Edmund Blunden speaks of the difficulty humans have in being realistic. Psychoanalytic studies have given, I think, the final answer to the question as to why the emotional factors important to the understanding of this problem have been neglected. It is because they are to a large extent unconscious.

The psychoanalytical theory came into being at approximately the same time as the modern atomic theory. A distinction, however, should be made between psychoanalytic theory and psychoanalytic practice. Psychoanalytic theory is the most comprehensive and general theory of psychology and includes a knowledge of and an exploration by a definite technique of the unconscious portion of the mental life which is actually much larger than the conscious portion. The consciousness has been compared to a flickering flame on the surface of the psyche, and the unconscious to that portion of the psyche comparable to the larger portion of an iceberg which floats underneath the surface, the visible portion of the iceberg being only approximately one eighth of the total mass. The psychic life roughly is somewhat like this in that only a small portion at any one time is conscious, while most psychic activity goes on beneath the level of consciousness.

In the unconscious there exist the forbidden and repressed instinctual wishes and forbidden memories and feelings which are held out of conscious awareness by psychic defenses. Psychoanalysis has permitted the scientific study of the unconscious, since a method has been devised to permit us to study and to understand the unconscious portion of the human mind, i.e. that portion beneath the level of conscious awareness. In addition, psychoanalytic theory constitutes the only truly biological theory of psychology.

The repressed material and instinctual impulses in the unconscious portion of the mind exerts a pressure to escape and frequently do so in disguised ways which cause harm to the individual and to society, as in those individuals with psychiatric illnesses such as neuroses, psychoses and criminal syndromes which cause so much suffering and so much loss to society and to the humans who make it up.

In contrast, psychoanalytic practice is the application of psychoanalytic theory to the treatment of psychic ills, and in this communication I shall deal largely with the relevance of psychoanalytic theory to an understanding of the phenomenon of recurrent mass homicide which, as I have said, rests on roots which are largely unconscious.

One of the most important consequences of the development of the psychoanalytic theory of psychic functioning has been a recognition of the psychic unity of mankind. That is to say that all humans are demonstrably human in their psychic functioning, no matter what color their skins, what part of the world they come from, and no matter what their ethnic background. They can all be demonstrated to have a common psychic unity and to be all closely related as human beings. This corresponds with the anthropologists' finding that all humans constitute a single species, there not being even a subspecific difference between them.

Thus human problems are human all over the world, and there are no exceptions to this rule. In the very short period of years in which the psychoanalytic theory has been in existence it has contributed significantly to certain important on going changes in society. Among these may be mentioned a progressive amelioration of the lot of those individuals afflicted with criminal tendencies, who formerly were cruelly punished without any appreciable effect on their criminality: to an elevation of the status of women and children; to the care of the helpless; and to a greater recognition of the crippling effect of psychic illness and of the need for proper treatment for those afflicted.

The discovery by psychoanalysts, beginning with Sigmund Freud and followed by Jones and others, of the vital role of the unconscious portion of the mind in human life, has been compared in importance to the discovery by Copernicus that the earth was not the center of the solar system because humans dwelt on it, and to the discovery by Darwin that man evolved from simpler living creatures instead of being a separate creation. Both of these earlier scientific advances produced a marked revolution in thinking, and the understanding of the unconscious portion of the human psyche has similarly produced a revolution in society and also an ongoing change in attitudes toward human beings and toward humanitarian endeavors. All three theories have been strenuously opposed by those groups who usually oppose change and progress.

Humans habitually resist the entry of unconscious material into the conscious awareness because of the painful feelings which are attached to the unconscious material, notably feelings of anxiety, depression or helplessness. Thus we expect, and indeed we find for this reason, a determined resistance to the comprehension of this important and relatively new method of approach to the study of the human psychic functioning. In this regard the remark of Bertrand Russell is pertinent. He said, "Most people would sooner die than think, and they not infrequently do so".

Sigmund Freud said that he disturbed the sleep of the world, meaning that after people became aware of what existed in the unconscious portion of the mind, they did not sleep as well for a while because of the anxiety which was aroused and which then had to be handled. The fact of the matter is that when we approach the study of the psychic life of humans unflinchingly we are forced to recognize that they are in fact the most aggressive and destructive of all living creatures, while inconsistently professing the most kindly motives.

I should only call to your attention the progressive destruction of the wild creatures, of the forests, and of the natural resources of the world; of the pollution of the air, land and water, and last but not least, the recurrent destruction of other humans in "wars" — all carried out by humans themselves. All of these tendencies make man a formidable enemy not only to other living creatures but to his own species. George Bernard Shaw, on viewing this spectacle, was moved to write, "I have never thought much of the courage of a lion tamer, but inside the cage he is at least safe from other men". In my communication, I shall take the position of John Donne who said, "Any man's death diminishes me, because I am involved with mankind".

What can be learned in relation to this problem of recurrent mass homicide from a study in depth of the human personality? We have discovered certain facts, for example, part of the answer to the question as to why men kill each

72

other. Why do they do it? In the waves of recurrent mass homicide, under the pressures of jarring ideologies, we recognize that the basic unconscious mechanism in each human being involved is necessarily the following: some hated image within the personality is projected outward onto a scapegoat, technically called a narcissistic object. This narcissistic object, or scapegoat, is then maimed or killed with the unconscious assumption that the internal conflict concerning hate and aggression will thereby be solved. Sadly enough the internal problem is never solved by projecting it upon an external human being and then maiming or killing that human being. Instead, as one can easily see, the internal problem is merely compounded and not in the least solved, more problems being created than existed before. Scapegoats of course have been utilized since earliest human history, and archaelogical findings demonstrate that scapegoats were sought out and murdered long before the dawn of recorded history. Does this historical fact signify that humans must inevitably continue this primitive kind of trial by combat, this attempt to solve pressing internal problems by maiming and murdering each other at intervals? It seems evident that they will be compelled to do so until the unconscious forces responsible for this terrible process are understood in all of their complexities and dimensions.

What takes place in recurrent mass homicide is somewhat as follows: One people attacks another people, the aggressors being frequently under the leadership of a severely disturbed, pathologically charismatic and narcissistic leader, such as the late and unlamented Adolf Hitler. We know that the narcissistic leader characteristically seduces the people of his country by lies, distortions of the truth, exaggerations and effective propaganda for the purpose of mobilizing their hate and aggression. A very primitive type of psychic reaction then takes place in them which allows him to convince a significant portion of the population of his country that they should give up their rights and privileges to him. Through seduction, terror, torture, murder and imprisonment, the leader then eliminates the leaders of opposition parties who frequently constitute the liberals of the country.

Once this is done, the country is committed to a suicidal course. Frequently a small and helpless nation is then attacked in order to try out not only the weapons but also the techniques of mass murder. If this succeeds, then a larger nation, more nearly equal in power, is attacked. The people of the larger nation then have no choice but to mobilize their military and industrial power, to use propaganda and even to copy the techniques of the enemy narcissistic leader in order to survive themselves, employing clichés, exaggerations and untruths about which I will comment later. I have already referred briefly to the economic, historical, sociological and military explanations for these phenomena, but to my mind they do not really adequately explain it; or rather they explain only part of the process, and I do not think that any one approach can give a total or complete explanation for this recurrent phenomenon, nor do I maintain that the psychoanalytic approach can explain all of it. I do claim, however, that it can explain an important and hitherto neglected part of it; and without this additional approach the other explanations will fail, as indeed they have failed, to give a full understanding of the process, which will finally enable us to prevent or to control it in a significant way.

Why does the narcissistic leader have to torture, to murder and to seize power to which he has no right? What does he want? This seems like a naive question, because it is perfectly obvious that he wants power, and I shall refer later to the unconscious origins of this drive to power.

From my observations made in Germany shortly after World War II, I do not believe that it is sufficient to say that Hitler gained power by terror alone. Seduction was an important technique in accomplishing this aim. The study of mobs, begun approximately 100 years ago by Gustave Le Bon, can give us some important data on the psychology of groups, a subject which the pathological charismatic leader intuitively understands and which he exploits effectively. Under the influence of a disturbed leader, Le Bon notes the individuals in a mob tend to regress to the level of the disturbed leader which, psychically speaking, is not a high level. Le Bon found that the individuals in a mob tend to behave in child-like ways, and they also tend to carry out atrocious acts, which as individuals they would not feel free to do and in fact could not do.

Sigmund Freud carried this study of group psychology further and showed that the functioning of the conscience structure of the individuals in a mob is temporarily suspended, and that a regressive type of identification with the disturbed and regressively aggressive leader of the mob permits the members of the mob to then commit inhuman atrocities under his leadership.

It seems clear that in time of war this phenomenon occurs on a large scale in the countries involved in armed conflict. Readers may recall wartime propaganda of World Wars I and II in which the "enemy" of the time was portrayed as a mob of subhuman beings, while the people of the allies were portrayed as superior humans. In this regard there is one wartime poster which is very illustrative. I refer to the poster with a portrayal of Uncle Sam, an elderly father figure dressed in the national flag who points his finger at the viewer, saying, "I WANT YOU! ". Now this command was a very difficult thing for a young man to resist, because the father figure, the source of the young man's conscience, was telling the young man that he wanted him to accept military service and possible death in defense of the mother- or fatherland. Many other psychologically significant and effective, but rather child-like propaganda methods were employed which incidentally were very effective in producing a mass regression to a less advanced level of psychic functioning.

The disturbed and pathologically charismatic leader who begins this process of mass aggression and homicide characteristically promises his people wealth, prosperity, and a better life when they have taken over the property of neighboring countries. He actually reserves the power for himself but he promises his people that they will share in his power, a promise which is never kept. Now why do power and wealth exert such a tremendously significantly effect on humans? I think we can only understand this if we refer to one of the most significant discoveries of Sigmund Freud, made approximately two generations ago.

Freud pointed out that the aggressive instinctual drive first became

74

manifest in a major degree in the second period of psychic development, the so-called anal phase which succeeded the first oral phase of nursing at the breast. In the anal phase the sphincter control is more or less forcibly insisted upon by the mother and is resisted by the infant, who resents the imposition of a new form of discipline which interferes with the pleasure of emptying his bowels where and when he pleases. Freud shocked the Victorians of his time when he conclusively demonstrated that an interest in money and power actually arose from the infant's interest in bowel sphincter control and in feces. The mother characteristically pleads with the child to empty his bowels, and then is often repulsed by the product because of its bad smell and its dirty character. The child is naturally puzzled by this contradiction, since the feces seem to him a precious part of himself, and he resents and resists this inconsistent attitude of the mother. I cannot go further into detail with this proof due to limitations of space, except to note that demonstrations of this phenomenon are an everyday matter to an analyst. I should only point out as additional evidence that, not infrequently, psychotic individuals believe their feces to be pure gold, this representing a regression to the infantile over-evaluation of the feces and of their later connection with the concept of money. The anal character who is not psychotic becomes quite frequently a very successful and powerful individual in Western society, this type of person often amassing large and sometimes huge sums of money and attaining positions of great power. We cannot escape the fact that Western society is basically an anally oriented society, which characteristically values power and money over human values. The phrase from the *Song of the Shirt*, "O God! That bread should be so dear, and flesh and blood so cheap", is as true today as when it was written in the early 19th century.

Indeed we must recognize the fact that money and power have been much more valued and are more precious to our society than human life or human liberty. People are severely punished for kleptomanic activities, such as stealing, although unconsciously they frequently are merely symbolically trying to take from society the love which was withheld from them in childhood. As a punishment their liberty is taken away for long periods of time and they are often ruthlessly discarded by society. If it is true that episodes of recurrent mass homicide are set in motion by a desire to gain money and power, as they seem to be, then we must conclude that young men of Western society are frequently murdered by the society for the gaining of money and power and that are often brutalized by being forced by the society to murder others. Today, with the recent invention of immensely powerful weapons, it is possible to murder whole populations in this mad search for power and money. There now is a growing protest, particularly on the part of young people, against this primitive value system and ideology which permits such atrocities and such inhumanity in the search for power and money.

The fact of the matter is that in any society which is basically anally oriented there must also exist a basic lack of stability, because of its being based on an unconscious and unhealthy vicissitude of an instinctual drive. This unhealthy basis engenders distrust and stimulates aggression and reaction in the society and, because of its basic inhumanity, repels thoughtful people who wish for a more humanitarianly oriented society.

A better understanding of the unconscious motives which produce recurrent mass homicide, the recurrent selection of pathologically charismatic government leaders, recurrent social and financial disasters, pollution of the environment, overpopulation of the world, racism with all of its consequent evils, and lack of an adequate food supply must be attained in order that populations will not be placed under such stress that they will again yield to domination by seductive, homicidal, narcissistic and pathologically charismatic leaders who will lead them to recurrent disasters.

If these are Utopian ideals then society is indeed in deep trouble. I do not believe that they are. I feel that we can achieve, through intensive interdisciplinary research, invaluable insights into all of these problems. But it is remarkable and significant that, while billions of dollars can be secured without difficulty for the development and manufacture of new and immensely powerful weapons, it is almost impossible to adequately finance research into the very matters which are dealt with in this lecture series.

What kind of person is the pathological, charismatic leader? In fact, individuals who set these vast mechanisms in motion for the purpose of securing power and wealth have been little studied. We do not have much opportunity to make psychiatric studies of pathologically narcissistic leaders for obvious reasons. Adolf Hitler was briefly observed by a German Army physician during World War I when he had developed some sort of psychiatric illness. He was diagnosed as "hysterical" by this Army doctor, who was not a psychiatrist. But when Adolf Hitler came to power, I am informed, this doctor suddenly disappeared.

I had the privilege of psychiatrically examining Rudolf Hess in Spandau Prison at the time of my visit to Berlin in 1948 because it was anticipated that he might make a third suicidal attempt. Although Hess was Hitler's deputy Führer and was the second highest person in the political hierarchy of the Third German Reich, in 1940 he surreptitiously stole an airplane and flew to the British Isles for the purpose, he said, of trying to persuade the British government to surrender to Adolf Hitler.

I had the opportunity of having a two hour interview with Hess, and to my surprise, I found him to be basically psychotic. He was definitely schizophrenic, and although he was a brilliant man, almost I believe in the genius class, he was all the more dangerous because of his psychosis and his intellectual brilliance. He had no access to the normal emotions of love and tenderness. Because of his extreme narcissism he could not believe that if something painful, such as torture, did not hurt him personally, that it could hurt anyone else. This curious and apparently contradictory pattern of traits freed him to commit atrocities on a large scale. It was my opinion that his psychiatric illness and personality structure must be very similar to Hitler's personality structure and illness, based on the similarity of their pronouncements, their actions, and their close cooperation in the production of Nazi tyranny with its horrifying atrocities, crimes against humanity and mass murders which characterized it.

76

In the early days of the Nazi movement Hess, together with Hitler, was responsible for the imprisonment, torture and elimination of German liberals and of the leaders of opposition parties which then committed Germany to a suicidal course leading to its destruction. It was shocking to me to find that the Deputy Leader of the most literate nation in Europe, who should have been recognized as being incapacitated by his psychiatric illness from holding any post of responsibility, instead was selected for one of the highest and most responsible posts, and ample evident indicates that this was also true of Adolf Hitler.

While I was on the staff of the Mayo Clinic as their Spanish speaking psychiatric consultant, I had the opportunity to interview Rafael Trujillo, among other political and military leaders of dictator-dominated nations of Latin America. Trujillo was at the time dictator of the Dominican "Republic", having been placed in this post by the United States. He alone was responsible for the extinction of liberty in the country of Santo Domingo, and he personally ordered the torture and murder of countless of his fellow countrymen. I found that he also was schizophrenic and was also without any access to normal guilt feelings and normal emotions of love and tenderness.

I was then stimulated to study the pronouncements and the actions of other dictators, such as Stalin, Mussolini, Napoleon, and Alexander the Great. To my great interest they all unmistakably showed the same characteristics which were so prominently demonstrated by Trujillo, by Hess and by Adolf Hitler.

They all clearly showed a callousness in regard to human life and human rights, as shown by their actions and not by their protests to the contrary, with which they endeavored to disguise their true motives and actions. They all showed an inconsistency between their pronouncements and deeds and they all demonstrated extreme untruthfulness. They all had a self-centered and fanatical belief in their "mission" to control their countrymen and eventually the entire world, even though this was thinly disguised as a beneficent desire to better their countrymen. They all demonstrated an extreme intolerance of opposition, which of course is a necessity in a democracy. They all exhibited great and callous cruelty, not only toward people of other nations whom they attacked and whom they used as pawns, but toward people of their own nations.

The Nürnburg Tribunal condemned many of the Nazi leaders to death because of their crimes against humanity. Hess was reprieved because he was a valuable propaganda prize and because, I believe, psychiatric observation during his capitivity conclusively demonstrated his severe psychiatric illness. Two years after my interview with Hess, I met the British psychiatrist who had had charge of him during his imprisonment in Wales after his flight to Britain. I learned that the British psychiatrist had also diagnosed Hess as schizophrenic but that he was forbidden by Winston Churchill to reveal this diagnosis because Hess would have had to be repatriated under the terms of the Geneva treaty if he had been diagnosed as having any illness, and Hess was too valuable a hostage to be repatriated. This psychiatrist also informed me that later, after Hess' second suicidal attempt, he was again forbidden to release the correct diagnosis because at that time the War Crime Trials would have been impeded. I was also forbidden by the American Military authorities to release my diagnosis on Hess because, I was informed, this would irritate the Russians, and at the time of my visit during the Berlin Airlift, the Russians were very easily irritated.

As a result of all these experiences, together with my own war experiences during which I had the opportunity. to meet and interview prominent and high-ranking military men, I was moved to make a sincere attempt to understand the phenomena involved and to dedicate myself to their study because of the danger to civilization and to the world.

During the war several soldiers in the combat zone asked the following question, "Why do men make war every generation? ". I later came across a similar reference in a book by Guy Gibson, the British pilot, who, you may remember, led the famous raid on the German dams which won him the Victoria Cross. Before his death in World War II he wrote, "Why must men make war every twenty-five years? Why must men fight? How can we stop it? Can we make countries live normal lives in a peaceful way? But no one has the answer to ;hat one". It occurred to me to try to ascertain if it could be true that wars do occur at intervals of twenty to twenty-five years. I was unable to find any accurate data about this so I compiled the intervals between wars in the following countries since the last quarter of the 18th century: the United States, Great Britain, France, Germany and Russia. I found that wars had occurred on the average of every 18 years in the history of the United States; 18.42 years in England; 19.85 years in France; 23.8 years in the history of Germany; and 17.74 years in Russia; the grand average for all countries being 19.56 years.

Now the period of late adolescence in humans extends from the 18th through the 21st years, and we recognize from psychoanalytic studies that this period constitutes one of the most critical periods of human psychic development. This is so because the individual is imminently preparing for adult life, and thus this period is always a stormy one from the standpoint of emotional development. It is also the period in which young men are drafted for military service in most nations of the world.

However, young men of this age are not allowed to vote in most countries. This is an interesting situation because if young men of this age group are assumed to be mature enough to be forced to fight, to kill and to be killed, to maim and to be maimed, but are not allowed to express an opinion as to whether the cause for which they are drafted to perform these duties is worthwhile, valid or invalid, then it seems that we have here a form of modern slavery, and I think there is no doubt about this.

In most parts of the world young men in this age group are forced into military service with the exception of a few peaceful societies such as the Hopi, the Arapesh and certain others. In almost all primitive societies young men are forced to undergo an initiation rite or ceremony in order to prove their masculinity, their fitness to enter adult life, their fitness to take a mate to reproduce. Some of these initiation ceremonies are very cruel, and, in fact, some are so cruel, notably the initiation rite of the Australian aborigines, that many young men die during the savage initiation because the penis is split with a stone

78

knife and many initiates bleed to death. In some tribes in New Guinea the initiation takes the form of a ritual head hunt or murder, or of war games in which many young men are killed.

In these war games no property or territory is won or lost, but young men fight and die as part of their initiation into manhood, ostensibly to show their bravery. As psychoanalysts we recognize that it is a more or less unconscious fear of not being masculine enough, and on a deeper level, an unconscious fear of castration which forces young men into these ritual murders, as well as on a more conscious level the fear of retaliation by the older males, social condemnation and ostracism.

Without going into further detail it is my opinion, based on my studies, that recurrent mass homicide is a disguised remnant of the ancient initiation ceremony or ritual of young men. Many of the primitive ceremonies involve mutilation of the male genitalia, and in primitive societies circumcision was originally carried out at the adolescent period as part of this initiation into manhood. This was later displaced to the newborn, this displacement occurring relatively recently in human history. In Australian primitives, as mentioned previously, a much crueler mutilation is carried out to this day. Recurrent mass homicide then may be considered as a remnant of the primitive initiation ceremony and is blindly carried out in each new generation, as soon as a new generation of males who have not been involved in the preceding war reaches the period of late adolescence. This occurs in Western society as a result of the unconscious impetus of the aggressive instinctual drive mobilized under the leadership of a pathologically charismatic narcissistic leader who recurrently starts the process.

We can now perceive some of the etiological factors which motivate and carry on, generation after generation, this plague of society which has devastated mankind since earliest recorded history. Millions of young men have lost their lives, many of great promise, in this purely emotionally motivated process which, from the intellectual standpoint, makes no logical sense whatever. These conclusions may seem surprising or shocking, but nevertheless they can be substantiated. They are not at present very well-known, simply because most facts about the unconscious mind are as yet not very widely known. It is also very difficult to make them known because, as mentioned previously, there is a strong resistance to their acceptance on the part of most people. As an evidence of this fact one can point to the difficulty in securing financial support for research into these matters, even though the preceding conclusions are based on scientific facts which analysts deal with every day.

What can we do from a so-called practical point of view to interrupt the vicious cycle of recurrent mass homicide which with the advent of hydrogen bombs and toxic gases now can destroy us? We must recognize, first of all, that the search for weapons of greater and greater power actually represents nothing more than the wish of the little boy, persisting unconsciously in the grown man, to obtain power superior to that of the father. Machines, including complex military machines and weapons, are nothing more than projections and representations of some function or organ of the human body. The computer, for example, is a rather crude representation of some functions of the brain, compared to which it is absurdly simple. The airplane and the guided missile have many of the features of the human body, including a brain, eyes, ears, and wings which of course in the bird are modified fore limbs, and so on.

We need more intensive interdisciplinary research on the whole meaning of weapons and of recurrent mass homicide as I have said, and this is an urgent need. Sigmund Freud, 50 years ago, wrote that there was not much time left for research into the unconscious motivations for war before the civilization would be destroyed or damaged beyond repair. It is now 50 years later, and very little progress has been made in this direction. We need to better understand many of the features of modern life which render people susceptible to domination by narcissistic, pathologically charismatic leaders, and one of these is an increasing tendency toward identification with machines. Machines, while they have produced many benefits to humanity, also have an unconscious impact on human beings, and indeed, an identification with a machine is an important disadvantage of their use. Machines are not human and they are not helpful objects for identification. But with the omnipresence of machines, a certain amount of this type of identification is inevitable. We must then provide more suitable human objects of identification for young people, and if possible, healthy ones and appropriate ones — not military men as has been traditional since primitive times.

As has been mentioned we need a better financial system and one which is not based on unconscious anality because this leads to so many abuses and to so much disturbance and injustice in society, since it is motivated from the unconscious and is not humanitarian in its basis. As long as we have an anally oriented society there must exist some doubt that we can completely interrupt the cycle of recurrent mass homicide because of a tendency to rate the value of power and wealth above human values.

Now I do not wish to be misunderstood. I do not believe that a simplistic economic causation of social movements alone exists. This is a naive oversimplification and the Marxist theory is oversimplified, in that it leaves out the emotional aspects of human motivation. The Soviet society would appear to be as anally oriented as is our own. There can be no question that if the emotional aspects of human armed conflict can be clarified and ameliorated, and if we can develop a system of economy which does not stimulate injustice, exploitation and murder of human beings, then such a society might be free from recurrent mass homicide.

But we have little time in which to work. A crisis which is approaching is nearly upon us. I refer to the overpopulation and the food shortage of the world. It is estimated that within 20 to 25 years there will be a world-wide and serious food shortage due to the rapid and dangerous increase of the population of the world. It is estimated that enough food cannot be possibly grown to feed the anticipated population unless this overpopulation can rather quickly be controlled, which is extremely doubtful. When this happens, the most powerful nations in the world will be called upon to decide who shall eat and who shall starve. Since the United States in now one of the two most powerful nations in the world, this need to decide life or death will not make us popular with less powerful nations. There will be objections to the decision as to who shall starve, and in various nations pathologically charismatic and narcissistic leaders then will inevitably arise to lead the people who are doomed to die; this phenomenon will occur as well in the powerful nations determined to keep what they have. Propaganda, the organization of nationalistic and violent political parties, seduction, terror, brutality and murder, will then again be used by the pathological leader to gain control, and then one can confidently predict there will ensue mass homicide unless some unforseen event happens or some scientific breakthrough takes place.

Unless we realize the danger in time, and through the proper employment of the scientific method do something effective about it, there will certainly be another explosion of mass homicide due to this cause, this time a more massive holocaust than any in previous history. This type of social stress always imposes severe stresses on education, culture, freedom of speech and an equal system of justice, and ominous signs are already present which could possibly lead to the extinction of these functions essential to a stable civilization. We have no choice but to exert every bit of our knowledge and every resource to avert another mass tragedy, because this time recurrent mass homicide, with the utilization of extremely powerful weapons, will inevitably and necessarily be mass suicide.

A final word about passive resistance is in order. The Yankee Thoreau advocated passive resistance to what he considered unfair governmental acts in prosecuting the Mexican War. Mahatma Gandhi learned much from Thoreau and created a new nation in India by the use of this technique. Dr. Martin Luther King, in our time, adapted the techniques of both Thoreau and Mahatma Gandhi and produced results in the political liberation of black people which undoubtedly could not have been obtained by any other means. It may be that this is really the only effective method of societal change in order to successfully oppose the rise of narcissistic charismatic leaders in their mad search for power and wealth, an evil to which an anally oriented society would appear to be predisposed. This technique is a desperate last resource, however, usually sought by people who are desperate and who have no other resource. There is no doubt that if it is carried out on a large scale it cannot be defeated.

Only an emergence from present ignorance accompanied with great dedication and determination by humanitarianly oriented people can save us from ourselves. Therefore an appeal to the conscience of the people of the world must be made in order to reverse the fatal trend in which Western society seems to be caught.

Finally it is essential to take cognizance of the extensive nature of the damage resulting from "recurrent mass homicide", called war, a damage which goes on for years after the killing stops. This is not evident to most people since it is usually hidden. We try to hide those whose lives are ruined through "wars" in Veteran's Hospitals, and those children who are physically and psychological-ly damaged in wars grow up to be susceptible to the processes taken note of in this communication. Thus, the damage caused by recurrent mass homicide is not all confined to people in hospitals, and the results of the brutalization and the suffering go on for years afterwards. We should indeed utilize every bit of knowledge in existence and, through organized research, try to gain more knowledge while there is yet time in an endeavor to stop this horrible, wasteful and suicidal disease of society.

BIBLIOGRAPHY

Freud, S. (1915), Thoughts for the Time on Life and Death, in J. Strachey and A. Freud (eds.), *Standard Edition of the Complete Psychoanalytic Work of Sigmund Freud*, Vol. 14, Hogarth Press, London, 1957, pp. 273—302.

Freud, S. (1932), Why War, in J. Strachey and A. Freud (eds.), *Standard Edition of the Complete Psychoanalytic Work of Sigmund Freud*, Vol. 22, Hogarth Press, London, 1964, pp. 199—218.

Freud, S. (1933), New Introductory Lectures in Psychoanalysis, in J. Strachey and A. Freud (eds.), *Standard Edition of the Complete Psychoanalytic Work of Sigmund Freud*, Vol. 22, Hogarth Press, London, 1964, pp. 7—184.

Freud, S., Group Psychology and the Analysis of the Ego, in J. Strachey and A. Freud (eds.), *Standard Edition of the Complete Psychological Work of Sigmund Freud*, Vol. 18, Hogarth Press, London, 1955, pp. 69—144.

Hughes, R.E., *The Progress of the Soul: The Interior Career of John Donne*, Morrow Inc., New York, 1968.

Jones, E. (1915), War and Individual Psychology, in *Essays in Applied Psychoanalysis*, Vol. 1, Hogarth Press, London, 1951, pp. 55—76.

Jones, E. (1915), War and Sublimation, in *Essays in Applied Psychoanalysis*, Vol. 1, Hogarth Press, London, 1951, pp. 77—87.

Jones, E., Can Civilization be Saved? , in *Essays in Applied Psychoanalysis*, Vol. 1, Hogarth Press, London, 1951, pp. 234—253.

Jones, E., Psychopathology and International Tension, in *Essays in Applied Psychoanalysis*, Vol. 1, Hogarth Press, London, 1951, pp. 301—322.

Le Bon, G. (1895), *The Crowd, a Study of the Popular Mind*, Fisher Unwin, London, 19th impression, 1920.

Russel, B., *Wisdom of the West*, Doubleday, New York, 1959.

Shaw, G.B., *Dramatic Opinions and Essays with an Apology*, Vol. 1, Brentanos, New York, 1909.

Walsh, M.N., The Historical Responsibility of the Psychiatrist, *Arch. Gen. Psychiatry*, (1964) 355—359.

Walsh, M.N., A Contribution to the Problem of Recurrent Mass Homocide, *J. Hillside Hosp.*, 15 (1966) 84—93.

Walsh, M.N., The Case of Rudolf Hess, a Specimen Study of a Narcissitic Leader, *Humanist*, 27 (1967) 49—51.

The Loneliness of the Long Distance Soldier

WALTER WILCOX

By way of introduction I would like to say first that there are two basic modes of describing things. One is through feelings, impressions, emotional reactions; another is through facts — descriptive, connotative words that try to express exactly what happened. As an illustration: if we want to learn about a hurricane, whom would we read? Joseph Conrad, with his vivid imagery — his interpretation of the massive, shrieking, living thing? Or would we go to the weather bureau's report to study the temperature, the pressure, the velocity, the eye of the hurricane? Probably if we want an accurate notion of what really goes on, we would do both. Both are valid ways of describing things. But we must sometimes make a choice, and the question arises tonight: through whose eyes do we describe the long distance soldier?

We have many accounts of the soldier: the moving portrait of Henry, the young soldier in Stephen Crane's *The Red Badge of Courage*; we have the accounts of Bill Mauldin's Willy and Joe, the symbols of the patient, weary, cynical soldier, mildly outraged by the indignity of war. We have Ernie Pyle, and we have others.

Or can we describe the soldier through dispassionate, statistical portraits as drawn by the behavioral scientists? One approach gives us the flavor and the feeling and the emotions; the other gives us the facts. In neither one alone does the true combat infantryman step forth. In the dramatic form we can describe one soldier or two or perhaps 12 (a rifle squad), but in the statistical portrait we can describe armies of soldiers. My choice tonight, because I think it is necessary to the *understanding* of war as opposed to an *attitude* toward war, is a factual portrait, in the hope that by some sort of dispassionate analysis of the soldier, we can cast some light on war and the human race. Much of my material tonight is taken from a cluster of studies entitled *Studies in Social Psychology in World War II* done by the Hovland group at Yale University. The evaluation of this material is entirely my own — in the light of my own experience and of observance of soldiers in action. (The interpretations are also modified by the fact that we know much more today, more than 20 years later, about how to interpret these data.) I have also chosen to limit my discussion to the combat infantryman, because in traditional warfare he is the person to whom the entire mobilization of armies is geared. And further, I have chosen the perspective of World War II because I know about World War II, and also for academic reasons: this is the war in which we had a long and sustained campaign which created the long distance soldier. And it is the only war for which we have exhaustive and detailed behavioral science data. (We probably have it for the Vietnam war but it has not been released.)

We are talking essentially about the combat infantryman. In a field army, the combat infantryman is very much of a minority. To give you a brief statistical notion of how much a minority he is: take an infantry division reinforced (by reinforced I mean with artillery and the other things that normally go with an infantry division — tanks, artillery and so forth). As it prepares for battle, in the classic deployment of traditional warfare, the division moves out into combat with only 96 men in the front from a total of 19,000 men. Later as the action begins and the formations coalesce, we have 536 men out of that total of 19,000 men actually in action or in one way or another engaged with the enemy. Still later, as the reserve units are moved up to replace other units, a maximum total of 2,816 rifle soldiers are involved in this 19,000 man division. Now if we add to that the number of troops in the rear and note the ratio of noncombatants to combatants, we find the infantryman in a distinct minority. (I might add for the sake of accuracy that in a defensive situation there would be more men involved.) But in a classic offensive situation, 2,816 men are actually involved in combat: that is, people who are individually expected to fight other people. Hence, right from the beginning, we find then that the combat rifleman is not only lonely in the psychological sense, but that he is more or less lonely in the numerical sense.

During World War II, the goverment commissioned a team of behavioral scientists led by Paul Hovland of Yale University, one of the leaders in the field of attitude measurement and research, to find out everything possible about the American soldier, particularly the front line infantryman, and more crucially, the long distance infantryman, the man who must campaign not just once but again and again. Some 75 behavioral scientists, their assistants and supernumeraries went into the field and began their inquiry. Much of my material tonight is taken from the results of this inquiry as interpreted by me. I'm sure that I will not do injustice to their data, but as their data are reported in a rather straightforward sense without too much interpretation, I think that from the perspective of time and the perspective of one who was there, we might get additional rewards from it.

It quickly became apparent as the study developed that the crucial question was: why does he keep going? What motivates a man, how can he rally his total psychological resources to face the indignities of war, what sustains him, what enables him to put up with the massive affront that endangers him at all times? To quote the work itself, (remember we are not quoting emotion-oriented material but from the work of a behavioral scientist), "a tired, cold muddy rifleman goes forward with the bitter dryness of fear in his mouth into the mortar bursts and machine gun fire of a determined enemy. A tremendous psychological mobilization is necessary to make an individual do this, not once, but many times". And to quote once more, this time on the sheer physical demands of a man engaged in this kind of activity, the report says: "rarely was the combat soldier subject merely to one kind of physical discomfort. His ills came in flocks. It's just not merely that he was cold and wet, but he was also deadly tired, dirty and without prospect of shelter. It is not only that his stomach staged a minor revolt against still another can of pork loaf, but he was simultaneously lying in a filthy foxhole under steaming heat and incessantly irritated by swarms of malaria-bearing mosquitoes". The effects of long continued multiple physical discomforts of this sort were intensely distressing, and if no relief were in prospect for an indeterminable future, they could seem to be well-nigh insupportable. The question is again asked, why did they do it? The behavioral scientist asked why would men do things like this — suffer the ultimate indignity in stresses and strains. And they resolved the question, as social scientists are wont to do, by asking the soldiers, and one question was: "Generally, from your combat experience, what was most important to you in making you keep going and do as well as you could? ". The results from today's perspective are somewhat clouded, and we must be rather wary of them. For instance, we know today that a respondent will answer according to what he thinks his questioner wants him to say. So really what we're dealing with here is a secondary analysis of the American soldier, produced by the people at Yale, but I think we find some very real and even more relevant information than they themselves extrapolated from their data. One finding looms large: those soldiers who responded aggressively (I mean in such terms as "hate for the enemy", "desire to kill"; the tough, mean soldier sort of thing) amounted to only 2%. I repeat that. Only 2% of all the soldiers responded in this context of hate, kill, meanness. And this, of course, is considered negligible. It fractures the naive notions of the belligerent and kill-oriented soldier. Even the motive of revenge, revenge for the death of a buddy, so prevalent in the superficial war movie, was totally absent in responses. I think we can safely extract from the data the reasons why. The death of a buddy to the soldier, the long distance rifleman, is an act of fate. It's just simply one more indignity of war. The enemy soldier who fired the shot is just another kind of infuriating annoyance in his world, a world that abounds in annoyances. In fact, it might be said, and I think fairly, that the enemy soldier who fired that shot probably has more in common, as we shall see, with the combat infantryman than he has with the noncombatans of his own kind. So once again, why then does he go on and keep going on?

In sorting out these findings, it is apparent that he himself is really not clearly aware of why he does on. Now his answers are vague, by and large. He says such things as: "Get it over with", and such things as "Not to let the guys down". And he says such things as "I don't even give a damn about *why* I go on; I'm too tired to care". He'll say such things as "Self-preservation, I don't dare do anything else". In short, he goes on because he must go on. And he sees nothing faulty about this circular reasoning; he merely sees no alternative. The researchers emphasize that the men found themselves in a new world; their old world, their homes, their communities, their families are now remote, they're misty; they're somehow static. They're frozen the way they were when he left. He can't envision his family changing, for he has had to create a world for himself, he and his fellow soldiers, a new world, a world of their own. And to quote from a study, "The isolation of the front line unit was such as to make the combat man feel completely set apart". To quote once more, "In a thousand ways, great and small, the soldier coming into the line had to find for himself a world that felt itself to be, and was in fact, removed physically and psychologically from all that lay behind it". His unit, the small group of men around him — they could range from the squad to the platoons, and even as high as the company at times — became his world. Behind him a great military machine inexorably continued to send forth supplies and men, but his unit lived and died apart from the other great world and the war. He knew that off somewhere to his right was another infantry division, the 4th division or what-not, and behind him, he knew there was a corps headquarter, the army headquarters, the army group headquarters, and the whole might of a nation. But they brought to him no sense of power, of massive solidarity. He knew about them, but he knew that his unit, so pitifully small and vulnerable, must function alone. Not all the power of the world's proudest nation could change the essential loneliness of this unit. For the men know — by now they know — the way in which the game of war is played; that this small unit will survive perhaps, or get sliced up perhaps, but only they themselves are involved, and this war for them is intensely local. Yet they do go on, and again we might ask, why?

But I think we have less and less hope of really finding out why. The researchers dealt with such things as the notion of implied force behind them. Are they being pushed from behind? Here we evoke the image, the old movie image, of the officer standing firm with the pistol in order to shoot any man who retreats. In point of fact, no man ever thought while he was playing his role of the threat of the shot in the back but then he never thought of retreating. The data show quite clearly that it never occurs to a man to challenge the military system (or seldom did he ever think of it). It wasn't his province to be expansive in his thinking — rules are rules, and any regulation that the army has, at this point in his life, is better than no regulation at all. He was pressed for answers as to why he did not challenge the establishment, the status quo, the army itself. And he is somewhat puzzled that anyone would even bother to ask him. It has never occurred to him. His answers, in response to questions of this kind, are purely routine and superficial. He would answer, "Well, I certainly wouldn't want a dishonorable discharge". (That was the most frequent comment.) "What would my buddies think?" or "I wouldn't want to let the folks back home down", or "I'd never feel like a man again" were other replies but not of significant frequency. He had to answer something, and this is what he answered because mostly he couldn't think of anything else to answer. He is bound to this lonely little group, psychologically, in that he has no other place to go. He doesn't dare leave them. Physically dangerous as it might be to remain, it is even more dangerous to leave. The single rifleman in the malestrom of war would have rough going indeed. So he stays and he goes on, and he goes on.

The power of this group allegiance and the desperate psychological need of one to identify with the others in his unit were demonstrated repeatedly when men would go AWOL from hospitals and other detached duty to rejoin their units. We don't know exactly why, but the suspicion is that the problem of psychological identity is so great within them that they couldn't bear the additional loneliness of not being with their groups. The loneliness in the unit sense was often expressed in a kind of mixture. There was a kind of poignant bitterness about their role, a sense of indignation that they had been cast in such a role, but yet mixed with this was a strong sense of loyalty to something, they didn't know quite what, and also a strong sense of pride. After all, these persons were the elite; they were a kind of curious mixture of the elite and the fall guy. And with certain bitterness they recognized this. Morale was not counted in terms of happiness with one's lot but in ability to endure, to accept a kind of stoic fatalism. And the infantryman's psychological world was bounded by a set of values expressed by what one talked about. Or, and probably more important, what one *didn't* talk about. For instance, it was taboo to talk about patriotism or love of country. It was carefully avoided. This was one thing you did not talk about. I quote one of the soldiers: "Ask any dogface on the line. You're fighting for your skin. A boy up there 60 days on the line is in danger every minute; he ain't fighting for patriotism". Another taboo is victory. It's not permitted to talk about or speculate on victory. Any speculation is sure to meet with a kind of cynical derision, probably a snort, perhaps followed by the usual four letter word with which infantrymen express themselves. Yet, and despite this, each knew that victory or being wounded (what they call the million dollar wound, a wound that is bad enough to keep one from coming back but not so bad as to be crippling) were his only hope. No units are going home; no units are being rotated out. These were truly long distance soldiers without any promise, implied or otherwise, that there would be any ending beyond victory or incapacitating wound or, of course, death. Each probably held the hope of victory within himself, but it was not to be mentioned. Bravery was another taboo. You did not talk about bravery. A comment from soldiers: "What do you want to be, a goddamn hero or something? ". Bravery was one of those things that was not mentioned, but soldierly skills — these were positive values, these were mentioned and discussed and considered to be acceptable. "That old boy sure can pull night patrol; he can see like a cat". Or, "Joe can play a tune with that automatic rifle." The skills of soldiering were indeed values that were adopted and I don't think that it's even necessary to explain why. They're there for survival. That was one of their primary values and one of their only values, or one of their few values.

The rear echelon which consisted of everyone beyond the range of machine gun and mortar fire was to be considered, referred to and thought of with disdain, contempt, and even with pity, the pity that man feels towards the half man. The very fact that the Navy and Air Force too were suffering heavy casualties to these soldiers was irrelevant. Theirs was a different war. They had their own world pegged now and were not really interested in what was going on elsewhere.

Another item they *could* talk about was fear. If a man broke under fire, he was to be treated tolerantly and with great compassion. Because there, but for the grace of God, go I. Fear was the sort of thing that was understood, and there were no sanctions, no bitterness against the man who finally succumbed to fear. Thus were the homely but vitally necessary sanctions concerning what was acceptable to talk about and what was unacceptable that these men defined in their small and alien world.

87

It has been said many times that the greatest loneliness that man can experience is that loneliness among people. We've all read about it, such things as the loneliness of the stranger at the cocktail party, the loneliness of the first day at a new school. Loneliness can exist in its most acute form when around people but unable to communicate with those people.

The behavioral science techniques employed in studies I've been citing here were not really sufficiently sensitive to probe for this inner loneliness. Yet, in the interviews, it surfaced quite frequently. One sentence of the report I think expresses it. It says: "Even in the midst of his fellows, each man had the inner loneliness that comes from having to face death at each moment". And another quote: "Personal survival taken for granted on a curious kind of faith up until combat, vanished in the realization that death might come at any time and that often it was more likely to come than not".

The fact of loneliness and the fact of fear have been said to be observable physically. I can give you such an example. Picture one of the units coming out of the line in what is called route march. A route march formation is two lines of soldiers moving down each side of a road, spaced out with enough interval to minimize any damage that might occur from artillery fire or an air attack. Watch these men as they move down the road and you will note that the faces are blank, expressionless, wooden. The company commander watches the men march past him — their eyes are veiled, that is they can see out, but no one can see in. They are remote, withdrawn, and there is no camera, despite all the news film we might take, that can capture the notion of these men who have managed in some way to conquer the tremendous psychological odds and to endure — it has a kind of a sound and smell and feeling.

The sketch that I've given you here has intentionally omitted the striking exceptions: the hero and the coward. Certainly such men were there, but what I've tried to do is deal in what we might call the great mass of people as defined by one standard deviation, that is the great group of people in the middle. The social scientists themselves say that there is no such thing as a maladjusted soldier; rather, there are maladjusted people who happen to be soldiers. It makes sense to strike the extremes from our portrait — certainly we have our Congressional Medal of Honor winners, and we have people who have fled. But, by and large, we're talking about those who make war possible. In this portrait one finds something weak and something strong; something weak and somehow pathetic in that the long distance soldier must practice a degree of self-delusion and reconstitute himself psychologically and even physically in order to survive. We find something strong and perhaps even noble, not in his willingness to fight again and again, but merely in his capacity to endure. When we look at the combat infantryman, when we try to grapple with war and the human race, we ask ourselves: of what value is it for us to know something about the combat infantryman? Does it in any way advance us in our understanding of war or the human condition? I think that indeed it does. I think there is even perhaps a slender ray of illumination. We ask: why does he go on and on and on against these fearful stresses, and we found, I think most important, it is *not* because he is filled with hate or that he is blood-thirsty or that he covets power. He goes on because given the task assigned him by his society, he just simply *must* go on. He can envision no other course of action. In no sense can any of the data, either personal observation or the behavioral science material, be interpreted to mean that war is his natural environment. Rather it is the opposite. It's about as unnatural an environment as possible. The answer, if any of course, to war and the human condition must be found really in some other arena. It's not going to be found in the natural aggressiveness of the combat rifleman. We've seen that man's capacity to endure as exemplified by the combat infantryman is almost limitless. And so the question essentially is a political or moral one.

We ask ourselves — who indeed has a right to ask these men to go and endure what they have to endure. It is not a psychological one, because we know indeed that they will endure.

I do have one more point before I close and open for questions, and I think it's worth mentioning. This is our system for choosing those people who will endure this combat. Among these infantrymen I've been talking about there was a noticeably significant proportion of Mexican-Americans and Indians. If we inquired further into it, we would find a relatively large proportion of what we call the underprivileged. Of course, at that time there were no Negroes in the infantry; that is, the standard infantry division. We did find there was a notable absence of Ivy League types in the infantry. The system, in short, was inequitable. And no one has proven to me — I don't think anyone has even suggested to me — that the Ph. D. candidate is more sensitive to the humanitarian values than the boy from the ghetto. In point of fact, I would suggest the opposite could well be the case. The boy from the ghetto could indeed be more sensitive to the values of life and of death than the Ph. D. candidate. I add this as an afterthought because I'm a realist. If we are indeed unable to abolish war, at least we might strive for a more just, fair and equitable distribution of the affronts and the indignations and the stresses with which war is associated. This might be a cop-out because I can't see war being abolished by us tonight or even by us in the near future. This is a kind of a plea for reform in how we go about a more equitable way of distributing this very onerous load.

Summary and Conclusions

MAURICE N. WALSH

In the human body and psyche there must exist, in order that they be in a state of health, a *homeostasis,* a state of relative balance or harmony *(homonoia)* between the various forces and drives of the body and psyche. Any factor disturbing this harmony produces disharmony *(eris)* in somatic or psyche functioning. This same dichotomy exists in the society created by human beings, serious disharmony in the society producing a state of imbalance dangerous to the lives and security of the human beings making it up.

This *homeostasis* in the somatic or psyche functioning of the human body and the *homonoia* or state of harmonious balance in human society cannot be considered a complete steady state, a condition which exists only in death. It is rather a balance of tensions, and as such is liable to disturbance by any imbalance between tensions.

The increasing cross fertilization between disciplines demonstrates the value of the point of view which regards the human as a biological organism reacting to the environment with the aid of inherited instinctual drives. His exceptionally large brain, however, permits an uniquely advanced learning process and a transmission of what has been learned through written records. This has resulted in the creation of a technology which has permitted an increasing degree of control of his environment.

The term instinctual drive here refers to a complex, stereotyped pattern of useful activity that is common to the species and is inherited and essentially unlearned. Recent biological research, however, demonstrates that an instinct is not fully developed at birth, and that some form of experience necessarily influences the development of the instinct. Thus, in the human and in other creatures, an instinct can be deflected, deviated, or perverted from its original biologically adaptive and protective aim and function. The human disturbances and deviations of the developmental process, due to the variable and frequently unfavorable environmental conditions operating on the infant, can produce a perversion of the aggressive as well as the libidinal instinctual drives, with the result that the aggressive instinctual drive can then be turned against others of the same species or against the individual himself, resulting in either homicide or suicide.

The blind influence of the predominantly unconscious portions of the human psychic functioning has promoted an increasing tendency toward alteration and destruction of the environment as well as of individual humans which has now become threatening to the continuation of the human species as well as of numerous other living creatures. The full awareness of this process has

90

been up to the present imperfect due to psychic defenses which prevent, to a large degree, unpleasant and unwelcome material from reaching conscious awareness.

However, due to this same ability to learn, the historical process and the nature of man and his instinctual drives has become progressively illuminated — this being importantly aided by the cross fertilization of disciplines of which the present work is a pioneer. The great plagues of mankind have to a large extent been eliminated through the application of the scientific method to the various activities and fields of human endeavor, but this method has not heretofore been applied to the plagues of recurrent mass homicide, pollution of the environment, racism and hunger; the latter resulting from mass overpopulation of the earth and from a delay in the application of scientific technology to the production of more food and to the limitation of human reproduction.

Intensive psychoanalytically oriented research into the phenomenon of the extensive suggestibility and gullibility of human adults is of basic importance in the prevention of the rise of aggressively perverted leaders to power. This gullibility and liability to seduction is basically and demonstrably due to a persistence of areas of psychic immaturity into adult life, rendering the individual liable to regression of his ego and superego functioning under the influence of a temporary identification with a persuasive pathological and charismatic leader who utilizes psychic regression and an appeal to the more childish elements in the personality to gain control. It will demand all of our acumen and our research ability to devise means of combatting this powerful tendency which is overt or latent in a large segment of the population, and the time in which to work is short.

The discovery of the technique of nonviolent resistance, which dates back essentially to Thoreau, the New England Yankee, who first practiced civil disobedience against unjust laws and social trends, merits our most close attention. Thoreau's technique was taken up by Mahatma Gandhi, who first applied it on a large scale and thus brought about the establishment of the independent Republic of India. In more recent times Martin Luther King has achieved results through the application of this technique which a short time before were considered hopeless of attainment, i.e. the freeing of the black population of North America from their bonds. This technique is thus worthy of intensive psychological research and understanding, and its application may well be necessary for the final abolition of the phenomenon of recurrent mass homicide.

The psychological implications of mass nonviolence as a method of resistance against injustice and exploitation are therefore important. The fact is that there is no effective retaliation against nonviolence except mass annihilation which is impracticable. Such retaliatory annihilation is so blatantly inhuman and sadistic that it can no longer be accepted by civilized people. Many individuals are alarmed and repelled by groups which advocate nonviolence because of its unfamiliarity and ist seemingly bizarre nature. It is, of course, true that it may be, but is not necessarily so, a means of turning aggression against the self in a self-destructive manner; but this does not and cannot detract from the major political importance of such a technique of resistance to mass murder in the modern world.

There is no complete agreement on all facets of the problem of recurrent mass homicide among the contributors, which is as it should be. Progress in science is made in large part through the asking of questions, followed by the thrashing out of satisfactory or alternative answers to these questions; and it is inevitable that specialists in the various fields should require satisfactory answers to questions involving their particular specialities. However, enough unanimity exists to suggest the outlining of at least a preliminary new modern theory for the occurrence of recurrent episodes of mass homicide, commonly referred to as war, which have devastated mankind like a recurrent plague from time immemorial.

The salient features of such a theory, together with the data on which it is based, may be outlined as follows:

(1) There is sufficient evidence to postulate in humans, as in other mammals, the existence of an aggressive instinctual drive which is basically adaptive and protective of the individual and thus of the species. This originally adaptive and protective instinctual drive may be deviated from its original purpose, as in ants and humans, in the absence of significant enemies of other species or predators, and perverted into mass attacks upon individuals and groups of the same species. These attacks must not be naively misconstrued as having the biological purpose of keeping the numbers of the species in question down. They rather represent a miscarrying of the originally adaptive and protective instinctual drive. In ants this has not resulted in any significant damage or threat to the existence of the species as a whole but with humans the situation is different. In the human the unusual and remarkable development of the brain and mind has finally resulted, in the middle of the 20th century, in the creation of weapons of such enormous destructiveness that the whole human species is threatened with extinction unless this largely unconsciously produced process of recurrent mass homicide can be understood and controlled before it results in the destruction of humanity.

(2) The occurrence of episodes of mass homicide, in nations of the Western world in recent human history, takes place at an average interval of 19.6 years, which is the time required for the arrival of each generation at late adolescence. It is in this period of life that the greatest psychic stresses are experienced, as shown by the fact that the suicide rate is higher in the late adolescent period than at any other stage of life, thus indicating the unusual intensity of psychic stresses at this period. The survivors of each "war" are less susceptible to the aggressive propaganda of pathological charismatic leaders than a new generation, which has not participated in a war, thus explaining the apparent "skipping" of adolescents arriving at this period of life between wars.

(3) The deprivation of civil rights of the late adolescent, that is to say the individual from the ages of 17 thru 20, is significant if it is recalled that males of this age group are called upon for involuntary military service in most peoples of the world without the opportunity to express themselves through the vote as to

92

the justice or injustice of the cause of which they are called upon to be maimed and killed, and to maim and kill other young men against whom they have no personal cause for complaint. This justifies the conclusion that we have here an abuse of individual freedom in this age group which needs attention and corrective action.

(4) The governing bodies and leaders of the nations of the world are made up predominantly of older males who recurrently produce mass murder, in recurring "wars", of younger males of each new generation who are, as noted above, deprived of civil rights. This would strongly suggest an intense and murderous, albeit unconscious, hostility of older males for younger males. This conclusion is borne out by the results of psychoanalytic research, as a result of which it is now recognized that the triangular constellation of the father, the mother and the son arouses hostile but largely unconscious feelings of great intensity in males which become repressed into the dynamic unconscious and continue to operate in hidden and concealed ways. The young male, being vulnerable in that he as yet possesses no civil rights and is furthermore less experienced and less able to defend himself, is the unfortunate object of this murderous but concealed and largely unconscious hostility of older males.

(5) The existence in the human of a significantly preponderant unconscious portion of the psychic life, in which reside the instinctual drives together with repressed traumatic memories, permits the human to act out in self-destructive, suicidal, and dangerous ways which now exist at a sufficient intensity, together with the invention of massive weapons of destruction, to threaten extinction of the species.

(6) The recurrent tendency of humans in times of stress to select leaders who are demonstrably aggressively perverted and psychiatrically abnormal individuals, who possess the power to seduce normal humans because of their peculiar absence of conscious guilt feelings, since normal humans have too many guilt feelings because of their predominantly overstrict conscience structures. This process permits the rise in each generation of brilliant but psychiatrically abnormal leaders who recurrently lead populations to episodes of mass homicide.

(7) Aggressively perverted leaders, such as Adolf Hitler, Mussolini, Stalin, Trujillo, Napoleon and Alexander the Great, under the pressure of their powerful unconscious homicidal and suicidal tendencies related to their aggressive perversion and psychic abnormality as demonstrated by Professor Walsh, arise in each generation and move into power vacuums, taking advantage of current historical, economic and sociological factors. Their uncanny ability, related to their intellectual precocity as well as their psychic abnormality, permits them to seduce large segments of the population into following them. Other less tractable segments of the population are subdued by brutalization, terrorism and murder so that the nations led by them are recurrently committed to a suicidal course of aggression, inevitably followed by defeat and destruction. In this process millions of innocents are sacrificed, murdered and lost without significant social gain.

This recurrent social process requires a multidisciplinary study for its complete understanding, and intensive further research is necessary for the complete comprehension and detailed working out of a solution to the problem.

An important contributing factor in the production of social disharmony is the "population bomb", *i.e.* the problem of overpopulation of the world. However, it is clear that overpopulation, serious as it is, is essentially related to an underproduction of food. When one considers that over one-half of the world's population exists in a state of partial or total starvation, while the richest nation of the world pays its farmers *not to produce food* in the interest of keeping food prices up, and also maintains a lower maternal and infant mortality rate than poorer nations, one can only wonder at the blindness and greed of such humans, who are indeed disregardful of the future welfare of their children. These will inevitably become the targets of resentment of other, more deprived peoples, resulting from the inhumanity of inflicting such a fate as starvation, psychological or physical maiming and death on the children of others. Modern scientific technology has been applied only minimally to the solution of this vital problem. Yet the Margaret Mead Foundation estimates that unless a serious and concentrated attack upon this problem is immediately made, widespread human cannibalism will ensue within 35 years due to massive starvation.

There is every reason to believe that unless the social evils of recurrent mass homicide, systematic starvation and overpopulation are solved through the scientific method applied without delay, the majority populations of the world will resort to methods of resistance in order to force such an application. These uprisings, it is to be hoped, will take the form of nonviolent resistance as applied by Mahatma Gandhi and Dr. Martin Luther King. But past history does not allow us to make such an assumption. With the rise in popular indignation under the pressure of murders of dissidents, widespread starvation and consequent maiming of the minds and bodies of children, one may confidently look for the rise of aggressively perverted, pathologically charismatic and narcissistic leaders who will seduce large masses of people into identifying with them and into sacrificing to them their civil rights. They will lead them again to aggressive action and to destruction, as have leaders of their type all through history.

It seems clear that only the following steps can finally result in the elimination of this recurrent and characteristically human plague of recurrent mass homicide, shared with humans only by ants:

(1) An effective world union of governments with a world police force devoted to the enforcement of laws and recognized by all members of the world governmental union.

(2) Removal of the profit motive from the armament industry and its extensive ramifications. This, like the removal of the profit motive from the purveying of narcotic drugs as is done in England, can exert a restraining influence on this industry in its purveying of weapons to dictator states.

(3) The creation of a new economic system freed from the unconscious anal influence which leads to an overvaluation of wealth and power because of the close association with anality (money is related to feces in the unconscious), and aggressiveness and destructiveness in present human society.

94

(4) Psychiatric examination prior to the selection of leaders, this to be done by a committee of nonpolitical psychoanalysts followed by periodic psychiatric as well as physical examinations to determine the fitness of the leader to continue in his post will inevitably become a necessity in the future in an attempt to avoid the seizure of power by psychically abnormal individuals.

The difficulty of acceptance of such a procedure by any population is self-evident. Yet if such a procedure is neglected, in the same sense that if a physical examination before selection of a leader with periodic physical examinations thereafter were to be neglected, then leadership by physically and/or psychiatrically unfit individuals is bound to sooner or later occur. This problem represents a major field for research and for dissemination of accurate information to the peoples of the world.

(5) Massive and continuing mutidisciplinary research projects into the above-mentioned factors which have created the episodes of recurrent mass homicide which have repeatedly devastated the earth; *i.e.* mass hunger, overpopulation, racism and pollution of the environment being given next priority.

It is of course evident that a situation of perfect harmony *(homonoia)* in human society cannot and will not exist. It is not beyond the bounds of possibility for a state of relative and less perfect harmony to be attained, however. In fact the continuation of human society *demands* that every effort we can make be applied to such an endeavor — we have no choice. The course of wisdom urges that we give a high priority to the initiating of such a massive research program backed with all the resources we can bring to it. Only then can we be relatively certain that our children will not be barbarously maimed, starved, murdered, or psychologically and physically warped and destroyed.

WALSH.   War and the human race